Scraptastic!

50 Messy, Sparkly, Touchy-Feely, Snazzy Ways
to Jazz Up Your Scrapbook Pages

Ashley Calder

Memory Makers Books
Cincinnati, Ohio

www.memorymakersmagazine.com

About the Author

Ashley Calder is an author and a scrapbook designer who has made her mark with appearances in several publications including Memory Makers Books *Pet Pages Unleashed, 501 Great Scrapbook Page Ideas* and *The Amazing Page*.

11 10 09 08 07   5 4 3 2 1

DISTRIBUTED IN CANADA BY FRASER DIRECT
100 Armstrong Avenue
Georgetown, ON, Canada L7G 5S4
Tel: (905) 877-4411

DISTRIBUTED IN THE U.K. AND EUROPE BY DAVID & CHARLES
Brunel House, Newton Abbot, Devon, TQ12 4PU, England
Tel: (+44) 1626 323200, Fax: (+44) 1626 323319
Email: postmaster@davidandcharles.co.uk

DISTRIBUTED IN AUSTRALIA BY CAPRICORN LINK
P.O. Box 704, S. Windsor NSW, 2756 Australia
Tel: (02) 4577-3555

Library of Congress Cataloging in Publication Data:
Calder, Ashley
  Scraptastic! : 50 messy, sparkly, touchy-feely, snazzy ways to jazz up your scrapbook pages / Ashley Calder.
      p. cm.
  Includes index.
  ISBN 978-1-59963-011-3 (pbk. : alk. paper)
  1. Photograph albums. 2. Scrapbooks. 3. Handicraft. I. Title.
TR501.C34 2008
745.593--dc22
              2007031869

Metric Conversion Chart

TO CONVERT	TO	MULTIPLY BY
Inches	Centimeters	2.54
Centimeters	Inches	0.4
Feet	Centimeters	30.5
Centimeters	Feet	0.03
Yards	Meters	0.9
Meters	Yards	1.1
Sq. Inches	Sq. Centimeters	6.45
Sq. Centimeters	Sq. Inches	0.16
Sq. Feet	Sq. Meters	0.09
Sq. Meters	Sq. Feet	10.8
Sq. Yards	Sq. Meters	0.8
Sq. Meters	Sq. Yards	1.2
Pounds	Kilograms	0.45
Kilograms	Pounds	2.2
Ounces	Grams	28.3
Grams	Ounces	0.035

F+W PUBLICATIONS, INC.
www.fwbookstore.com

Editors: Stefanie Laufersweiler, Kristin Belsher
Designer: Marissa Bowers
Art Coordinator: Eileen Aber
Production Coordinator: Matthew Wagner
Photographers: Christine Polomsky, Tim Grondin
Stylist: Jan Nickum

Dedication

I dedicate this book to my two sweet girls, Summer Lily and Addie Blue, who light up each day and make our home joyful and my heart happy. None of this would have been possible without you. To my mom, my sister, and my dad: I love you all. And to Paul, who always believed in me, who is always happy for one more trip to the art supply store, and who leaves perfect cups of coffee on my desk; thank you for your continual encouragement, thank you for your honesty and enthusiasm for everything I do.

Acknowledgments

Thank you to Memory Makers Books for extending this most wonderful opportunity to me. Thank you to my amazing editor, Christine Doyle, who never ceases to astonish me with her vision for this book, her creativity, and patience in answering all of my questions, big and small. Thank you to my talented graphic designer, Marissa Bowers, who made this book as beautiful as it is. Thank you to Christine Polomsky, my excellent photographer, for making my projects shine, her enthusiasm, and gentle reminders to please sit down. Thank you to all of the other folks at F+W Publications who have played a part in making my book dreams come true.

Introduction **6**

Chapter 1: Messy 8

Chapter 2: Sparkly 42

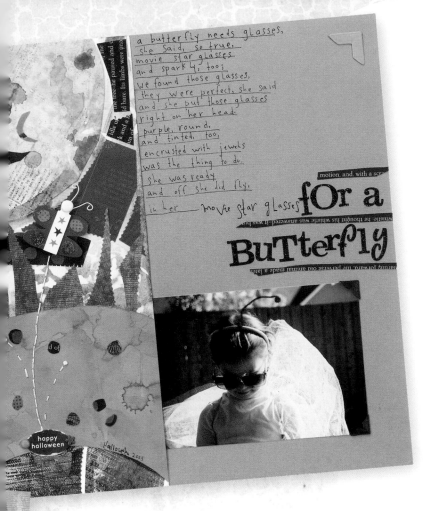

Chapter 3: touchy-feely 64

INTRODUCTION

Have you ever looked at a painting hanging in a cafe and sighed, "I wish I knew how to do that"? Have you seen an embroidered pillow in your favorite boutique and thought that it would make a great layout? Or maybe you've studied your gorgeous gold jewelry, or the perfect glittery touches on a birthday card, and wondered how the metallic and sparkly finishes could be easily replicated. Perhaps you're just ready for something new to add to your layouts and you don't know where to start. If any of these statements sound like you, here's some great news—you can do these things! Now! Even if you have no prior experience with painting, even if the thought of stepping into an art supply store or threading a needle makes you weak in the knees, you can do it! The clear step-by-step photos and captions that illustrate each technique will show you exactly what to do and how. All you need to add is a willingness to experiment and enjoy yourself.

So gather together all those supplies you've always wanted to play with and instead of asking, "How?" or "Why?" ask yourself, "Why not?" Why not try something new today? Why not do something you've always wanted to do? Why not play and have fun?

CHAPTER ONE

Messy

Walk into an art store and suddenly you're surrounded with the messy stuff: pastes, paints and printing supplies; acrylics, inks, watercolors; masking fluid, masking tape; clays, glaze and artist's crayons. It may seem overwhelming, but it doesn't have to. Art supplies were made to be used, and we shouldn't be afraid to play with them. So step through the projects in this chapter and get to know your new messy friends.

Left in right,
they fit together
hand in hand
and complement each other
well.

She asks; she answers.
She takes; she gives.
She runs; she follows.

Our two girls,
sweet each in their own way,
they go together
apart and one,

Counterbalanced
Like night and day.

Valen's Aug06

"Messy" Watercolor

I LOVE THE UNIQUE QUALITIES OF WATERCOLOR, particularly the beautiful way the transparent layers dry, and the uneven edges left by pooling paint. I especially enjoy creating "messy" watercolor pieces in which the paints are encouraged to pool, drip and blend together.

Experiment with combining layers of wet or dry paint. (Though, I prefer to let individual colors dry between layers to avoid the brownish "mud" that can result when certain ones mix too much.) Leave brushstrokes alone once applied, or use a water-moistened brush to soften hard edges. Affect the watercolor in a variety of different ways by incorporating additional mediums such as masking or gesso.

PAGE SUPPLY LIST

Watercolor paint and paper (Winsor & Newton); watercolor tape; patterned paper (Karen Russell, Prima); rub-on letters (K&Co.); stamp (Sugarloaf); stamping ink (Stewart Superior); frisket film (Artool); gesso (Liquitex); metal frames (Maya Road); brads (Making Memories); floss (DMC); journaling tabs, photo corners (Heidi Swapp); pen

For this technique,
you'll need:

Watercolor paper

Brown paper tape

Support board

Watercolor paint

Water

Palette

Brushes

White gesso

Frisket film (optional)

1 ATTACH THE PAPER TO ITS SUPPORT

Cut the watercolor paper to size, leaving a quarter-inch (7mm) allowance on each side, and place it on the board. Tear a piece of brown paper tape to the length of each side. Moisten the back of the tape with a wet paper towel and affix the paper's edges to the board.

2 PREPARE THE PAINT

Squeeze a bit of tube watercolor onto your palette. Mix water into the paint using your brush. (Do this with any watercolor you use, so that the paint will flow on your paper.)

3 APPLY MASKING, THEN BRUSH ON THE COLOR

Apply masking if desired. Here, I cut the letters of my grandfather's name out of frisket film and applied them to the watercolor paper (see page 34 for this technique). With paint and a generous amount of water on your brush, paint broad strokes of color onto the paper. Work quickly and freely. Allow the watercolor to pool in different areas to create a darker tone when the paint dries. »

11

★ Choosing Watercolor Paper

I like to use 140 lb watercolor paper for my projects. So all the projects in this book (unless otherwise noted) use 140 lb paper. Watercolor paper is available in cold press, hot press or rough press. Choosing a press is really a matter of personal preference, so try out different presses and go with what you like. ★

4 DROP ON SOME COLOR

To make drips, hold the brush above the board and squeeze the bristles. Let the watercolor dry.

5 ADD GESSO FOR TEXTURE

Pour a pool of watery, white gesso near the bottom of the page. (See page 17 for details about gesso.) Create additional texture by dipping an empty bottle into the gesso and stamping it on the paper.

6 ADD ANOTHER COLOR

Brush, drip and spatter another paint color on the top left corner of the page. To spatter, tap the handle of your loaded brush against your hand or another brush as you hold it over the paper. Let it dry.

7 APPLY MORE COLOR, THEN REMOVE THE MASKING

Drip a third color onto the top right corner of the page; tilt the board so the paint flows down the page. Once all the paint has dried, remove the frisket film mask.

Add Messy yet Delightful Touches

However messy you like watercolor, it doesn't have to be done in a page-covering way to be effective. Here I used a very small amount of gesso and watercolor, stamping it with a film canister lid and letting it creep up and across the page. Even a bit of spilled paint on your page can give it a fabulously artistic touch!

PAGE SUPPLY LIST

Cardstock; iron-on accents, letter stickers, patterned paper, rickrack, sticker accents, tags (SEI); floss (DMC); gesso (Tri-Art); watercolor paint (Winsor & Newton); photo corners (Canson, Heidi Swapp); brads; concho (Scrapworks); watchglass (unknown); adhesive foam; pen and ink (Speedball)

A Note about Brushes

For most of my projects, I use either old brushes or inexpensive brushes from the dollar store. This way I can abuse my brushes and be as messy and rough as I need to be without the worry of ruining a good brush. Unless otherwise specified, you should use stiff-bristled brushes for the projects in this book.

Watercolor on Yupo Paper

ONE OF THE UNIQUE PROPERTIES OF YUPO PAPER—which is, in fact, made of plastic—is its inability to absorb paint as traditional watercolor paper does. Because the paint sits on the surface rather than being absorbed, the result is more vibrant color and paint that can easily be manipulated and reworked. Yupo can be painted on like regular watercolor paper, but common household items can be applied directly on top of wet watercolor to create a variety of eye-catching effects for your pages. Sprinkling salt will result in a mottled, grainy texture; plastic wrap makes delicate lines and the appearance of folds in the paper.

PAGE SUPPLY LIST

Watercolor paper (Yupo); watercolor paint (Winsor & Newton); patterned paper (Karen Foster); journaling accents, letter stickers (Heidi Swapp); rub-on accents (Christine Adolf); decorative scissors (Provo Craft); photo corners (Canson, Heidi Swapp); pen and ink (Speedball)

1 DAMPEN THE PAPER AND ADD PAINT

Secure Yupo paper to the board with loops of transparent tape or glue dots on the back, then dampen it with a wet paper towel. Mix the watercolors on the palette. Because the paint will naturally mix under the plastic wrap (in Step 2) during the course of drying, it is best to avoid using colors that could create muddy browns if mixed. Blue, for instance, would be better paired with a like color such as green rather than orange, an opposite color. Wipe and drop multiple colors onto the paper.

2 COVER WITH PLASTIC WRAP

Cut a piece of plastic wrap approximately the size of the paper and gently place it over the paper. Cut another piece to cover the rest of the paper, if needed. Set the board aside to dry completely (this may take overnight or even two days). Lay it flat and avoid disturbing the plastic while the paint is drying.

3 REMOVE AND REVEAL

Once dry, gently remove the plastic wrap to reveal the effect.

For this technique, you'll need:

Yupo paper

Transparent tape or glue dots

Support board

Watercolor paint

Brushes

Palette

Water

Plastic wrap

15

Working with Yupo

* The edges don't need to be taped down prior to painting. *Yupo won't buckle or warp under the paint. If you want to hold the paper in place while you work, secure it with tape loops under the four corners.*

* Be sure to handle your unpainted paper with freshly washed hands. *The natural oils in your fingers can mark the paper and those areas will resist any paint applied. Yupo can be washed with a diluted soap-and-water solution to clean any fingerprints.*

* Due to the impermeable nature of Yupo, dry or wet watercolor can be easily washed off the paper. *This makes it easy to fix any mistakes or areas with which you may be unhappy.*

* Finish your Yupo artwork with a fixative spray. *Handling it with damp fingers may lift paint from your page. A fixative spray like Krylon works well.*

Crackle Petals

I INADVERTENTLY DISCOVERED THIS AGE-OLD CRACKLE TECHNIQUE when I was a little too messy with liquid glue on a project I would later paint. The resulting cracks in my topcoat of paint were a very happy accident! A flexible bottom layer of glue creates crackles in a rigid top layer of paint as the paint dries.

Experiment with different thicknesses of glue and paint, diluting the glue with a bit of water or dishwashing detergent if it does not spread pleasantly. When adding the paint, be sure not to go over any sections more than once, or the crackles will be disturbed.

PAGE SUPPLY LIST

Cardstock; buttons, patterned paper (Autumn Leaves); chipboard letters (Heidi Grace); flowers (Prima); photo corners (American Crafts); rhinestones (Westrim); chipboard accents (Technique Tuesday); rub-on accents (Chatterbox); glue (Aleene's); gesso (Tri-Art); pen (Marvy)

1 **SEPARATE PETALS FROM A FLOWER**

Remove the plastic stems from a silk flower and take the flower layers apart. With scissors, cut some of the smaller flower petals from the layers. (The smaller petals are rounder than the larger ones, and add more dimension to a layout.)

2 **GLUE THE PETALS IN PLACE**

Cut a 2.5-inch (6.35cm) circle from cardstock. Use tacky glue to glue the petals to the cardstock, overlapping the petals slightly.

3 **BRUSH THE PETALS WITH GLUE**

With a wet brush, slightly water down the glue. Brush the glue onto the petals, covering them. Allow the glue to dry.

4 **ADD GESSO**

Paint white gesso (see sidebar) or acrylic paint over the flower petals with a wet brush and let it dry.

17

All about Gesso

Gesso was traditionally prepared by mixing calcium carbonate with a glue. Modern gesso is a compound made from acrylic polymer and calcium carbonate. Gesso has a texture that provides "tooth" for the next layer of paint to grip. Gesso can be applied to a variety of surfaces—like canvas, cardstock, clay and wood—to prime them for painting. It can accept several types of mediums, including acrylics, oils, watercolor, liquid inks, dry pencils and stamping inks.

Acrylic Paint as Adhesive

she'd float all day
and float all night
she'd float away
into that blue lake.
thought she'd float
clear across the sea.
waves and fishies
in her wake.
under hot sun and
prone to buoyancy
she'd float out

on her salty ride.
round the world
on the cusp of the tide.
floating, floating,
floating once more
and she'd float back

to the

Lake

shore.

MATTE POLYMER, a common adhesive used in collage and mixed media pieces, is essentially pigmentless acrylic paint. Like its clear counterpart, acrylic paint can be used to hold a variety of small, lightweight items in place, such as stamps, pebbles or beads. A light covering of acrylic paint is also the perfect way to adhere a transparency (as shown in the layout on this page, in the arch made from a preprinted transparency and yellow acrylic).

Acrylic gesso can be used in the same manner. Experiment with the paint thickness and the item weight required for acrylics to work as adhesive.

PAGE SUPPLY LIST

Watercolor paper (Winsor & Newton); acrylic paint (Curry's, Tri-Art); acetate (K&Co.); chipboard letters (Maya Road); rub-on accents (Fancy Pants); postage stamps; shells; pebbles; glitter (Stix2Anything); pen and ink (Speedball)

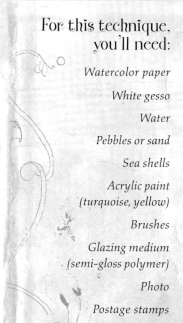

For this technique, you'll need:

Watercolor paper

White gesso

Water

Pebbles or sand

Sea shells

Acrylic paint (turquoise, yellow)

Brushes

Glazing medium (semi-gloss polymer)

Photo

Postage stamps

1 ADHERE WITH GESSO

Thin white gesso with water and pour a puddle along the top-right corner of the layout. Sprinkle sand or pebbles into the wet paint and tilt the paper to allow the paint and sand to run down the page slightly.

2 AFFIX THE SHELLS

Place a thick line of gesso on the page and press three large shells into the paint. Adhere only the bottom of the shells to slide a photo under once the paint is dry.

3 PREPARE THE ACRYLIC PAINT

If the turquoise acrylic is too thick, thin it slightly with glazing medium (see page 20 for instructions). Then pour the paint into two puddles on the paper.

4 ADHERE ITEM

Set old postage stamps with boat images into puddles of turquoise acrylic so only the bottom portions of the stamps are adhered and the tops float free.

19

Glazing Medium

SEMI-GLOSS POLYMER IS AN ACRYLIC MEDIUM used to create transparent glazes when mixed with acrylic paint. By varying the amount of acrylic paint and acrylic polymer, it is easy to achieve a variety of finishes from light tints (made with lots of polymer and a touch of acrylic paint) to more heavily pigmented glazes (with more acrylic paint and less polymer). I prefer to use heavier watercolor paper for a glazing surface, as it holds thick paints well without buckling or warping. The effect of glazing is a dimensional finish that shows much more depth and richness than a flat coat of acrylic paint.

PAGE SUPPLY LIST

Watercolor paper (Winsor & Newton); acrylic paint (Curry's, Tri-Art); semi-gloss polymer (Tri-Art); chipboard letters (Scenic Route); rub-on letters (KI Memories); photo corners (Heidi Swapp); sticker accents (Making Memories); floss (DMC); brush marker (Marvy); pen (Sakura)

1 COVER THE PAPER WITH PAINT

Cut a piece of watercolor paper, leaving a quarter-inch (7mm) border on all sides. Secure the paper to the support board using brown paper tape. Paint a background with pink acrylic and a wide flat brush. Don't try to be neat; allow the brushstrokes to show. Let it dry.

2 ADD GLAZING MIXTURES

In a small bowl, mix two parts glazing medium (semi-gloss polymer) with one part pink acrylic. Brush the mixture over the background, smoothing out most brush lines but leaving some texture in place. Let it dry. Mix the glazing medium with crimson acrylic (3:1 ratio) and paint this onto the surface randomly, keeping the paint toward the edges of paper.

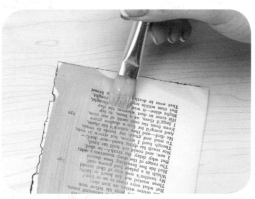

3 APPLY WHITE GLAZING MIXTURE

Mix a very small amount of white acrylic with glazing medium (1:4 ratio). Fill in the center of the paper with the white-tinted glaze. Dip the brush in water and drip a few drops of white onto the page. Set it aside to dry.

4 GLAZE A TORN-OUT BOOK PAGE

Mix glazing medium with yellow acrylic (3:1 ratio). Paint an old book page with the yellow glaze and leave it to dry. Then cut the book page into small strips and adhere it to the pink-and-white glazed paper with acrylic glazing medium.

Texturizing Medium

SURFACE TEXTURE INSTANTLY TAKES FLAT PAGES to the next level of visual interest and depth. One way (perhaps the easiest) to do this is to apply a texturizing medium such as nepheline gel or modeling paste. Both are acrylic mediums capable of holding fine detail and also acting as an adhesive. Because they are artist-quality, they hold up well and generally will dry without cracking or peeling.

Nepheline gel is usually reserved for mixing with acrylic paint to add a grainy texture, but it can be applied directly to the page for a raised, sandy title. The gel's translucent quality provides an intriguing alternative to traditional lettering. Modeling paste, typically used for adding crisp texture and rigid peaks, is nearly limitless in textural possibilities as it can be carved and sanded once dry.

PAGE SUPPLY LIST

Cardstock; gesso, modeling paste, nephaline gel (Tri-Art); letter stickers (K&Co.); dried flower seed heads, muslin, rusty nail, vintage lace , newspaper clippings (unknown); AL Fat Boy font (Internet download)

For this technique,
you'll need:

Cardstock

White gesso

Brush

*Muslin, trimmed
to fit 12-inch
(30.5cm) cardstock*

Modeling paste

Wooden craft stick

*Items to press
into the paste
(such as dried flowers)*

*Nepheline gel
(extra coarse)*

Stencil for letters in title

1 SPREAD GESSO AND APPLY MUSLIN

Spread white gesso over the cardstock with a brush. Place the muslin over the gesso on the cardstock and smooth into place. Brush more gesso onto the muslin to get fairly even coverage (although having a few uncovered places is fine). Allow the gesso to dry.

2 ADD MODELING PASTE

Apply modeling paste randomly to the muslin using a wooden craft stick. Use the stick to create texture with the paste.

3 PRESS INTO THE PASTE

While the paste is still wet, you can press objects, such as mesh, into it to create additional texture.

4 ADHERE OBJECTS

Apply more paste to adhere other items to the page, such as a dried flower.

5 FILL IN A STENCIL WITH GEL

Print out large block letters onto cardstock. Cut out the letters and use the cardstock as stencils. Place a letter stencil on the layout and fill in the stencil with the nepheline gel using a craft stick.

6 LIFT BEFORE DRYING

Once the letter is filled and the gel is still wet, lift up and remove the stencil. Repeat for the other letters in the title.

23

Stamped and Painted Clay

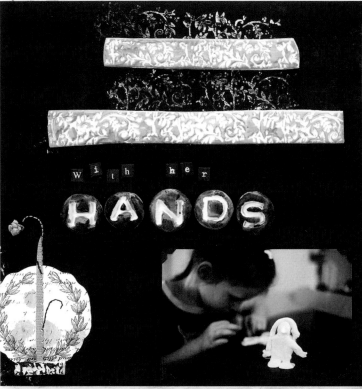

AIR-DRY CLAYS CANNOT BE MATCHED FOR EASE OF USE, and their ability to accept a variety of media—including watercolor, acrylic paint, inks and crayons—makes them a versatile product with countless possibilities. Because air-dry clay is lightweight, pages containing handmade clay accents will not weigh down your albums. Plus, you have total control over the thickness of your clay creations, whether your preference is bulky or thin. A bit of thick, tacky glue will adhere the small clay shapes to the page.

PAGE SUPPLY LIST

Cardstock; patterned paper (7gypsies, BasicGrey, Scenic Route); modeling clay (Crayola); acrylic paint (Curry's, Tri-Art); watercolor paint (Winsor & Newton); gesso (Liquitex); letter stickers (K&Co.); stamps (Leave Memories, Magnetic Poetry, Purple Onion); labels (Making Memories); photo corners (Canson); floss (DMC); ink (Clearsnap)

Experiment with Shape

Don't limit yourself shape-wise when it comes to using clay on a page. In addition to small, round accents, try adding long stamped and colored strips.

1 FLATTEN CLAY FOR STAMPING

Break off a small piece of air-dry clay and roll it in your palms until it forms a ball; continue rolling to smooth out any lines or seams. The ball should be approximately 1 inch (2.5cm) in diameter. Gently flatten the ball into a disc shape using your fingertips, taking care to flatten evenly. I flattened my discs to approximately a half-inch (13mm) thick, but if you care for less bulk on your projects you can make the discs thinner (and the letter impression would not be as deep).

2 STAMP THE CLAY

Press one letter stamp into each flattened disc. Use firm, even pressure. Carefully peel the disc from the stamp. I have never had a problem with the clay sticking to the stamps, but if you find your stamps are not releasing from the clay, simply dust your stamp with cornstarch before making an impression in the clay. Leave the clay out overnight to dry.

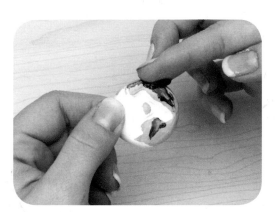

3 ADD COLOR

To color the clay, simply put a small amount of yellow acrylic on your fingertip and quickly work the paint over the surface of the disc. Avoid filling in the recessed letter image with paint.

Once the first coat of yellow acrylic has dried to the "just tacky" stage, go over the surface of each disc using a small amount of crimson acrylic. I prefer to work quickly and messily, leaving the paint coverage imperfect and textured.

Scratch Print

SCRATCH PRINTS ARE A SIMPLE MEANS OF RE-CREATING the messy, linear look of printmaking at home with little investment in special materials. The basis of the process is simple: a thin layer of printing ink is topped with printing paper that is backed with a copy of the image to be re-created, and the pressure of tracing the image with a ballpoint pen then transfers the ink to the printing paper. The final print will be the mirror image of the picture you trace, so be sure to flip horizontally any images containing writing to maintain proper orientation of the letters.

Turn a piece of your child's previous artwork into a print, create an original piece of art yourself, or give the pen to your child and have your little artist create a one-of-a-kind work of art for your album. A special thanks to my friend, artist Jean Leider, for teaching me this technique.

PAGE SUPPLY LIST

Watercolor paper (Winsor & Newton); brayer, printing ink (Speedball); placemat (unknown); patterned paper (Scenic Route); chipboard letters (Heidi Swapp); plastic stars (American Crafts); decorative pins, ribbon, tags (Heidi Grace); decorative scissors (Provo Craft); stamps (Sugarloaf); ink (Stewart Superior); pen (Sakura)

For this technique, you'll need:

Child's artwork

Tape

Watercolor paper (slightly larger than artwork image)

Water-soluble printing ink (black)

Plastic placemat

Brayer

Ballpoint pen

1   PREP THE ARTWORK AND APPLY THE INK

Make a copy of the child's artwork and tape it to the center of a piece of watercolor paper with the image facing up, and set aside. Squirt ink on the placemat. (For this technique, I use an inexpensive, thin plastic placemat, as it gets covered in paint and can easily be replaced.)

2   ROLL THE INK

Using a brayer, roll the ink on the placemat into a thin layer.

3   TRACE THE ARTWORK

Gently lay the watercolor paper (blank side down) onto the inked placemat, taking care not to press the paper into the ink with your fingertips or hands. Trace over the artwork using a ballpoint pen.

27

4   REVEAL THE PRINT

Once the image is fully traced, lift the print at the corner and peel the paper off the ink. Lay the print flat to dry.

Scratchwork with Artist's Crayons

SCRATCHING OR ETCHING INTO CARDSTOCK and filling in color with artist's crayons is a fun alternative to traditional means of drawing. Artist's crayons are heavily pigmented wax pastels, and although they are an artist-quality medium, they still maintain that wonderful grade-school look of wax crayon. Artist's crayons are soft, and if used gently on the surface of the paper, the etched line in the cardstock will not fill with pigment—leaving behind an outline of the image in the color of your cardstock. If you prefer additional contrast between the etched lines and the surrounding color, trace along the lines with an inkless ballpoint pen after coloring the image.

PAGE SUPPLY LIST

Cardstock; artist's crayons (Caran d' Ache); photo corners (Canson, Heidi Swapp); stylus; pen and ink (Speedball)

1 SCRATCH ON THE DESIGN

Scratch a design onto untextured cardstock (or the untextured back side of textured cardstock) using a metal stylus. Press firmly enough to leave a deep indentation, but take care not to tear the paper.

2 ADD CRAYON TO REVEAL ETCHING

Using the side of a crayon or holding it on an angle, gently fill in color on the cardstock to reveal your etched design. Layer colors for greater dimension. Here, I'm using a bright pink to highlight the heart.

3 TRY SMUDGING

Finish coloring with various colors. If you like, smudge some of the colors with your finger for a different effect.

29

Scratch into a Surface Colored with Crayon

Color multiple layers thickly with different crayons over plain cardstock, then color a top layer with black crayon. Use a metal stylus (or inkless ballpoint pen) to etch a design; the top layer of black crayon will peel off, revealing your pattern in the intense colors of the crayons beneath.

CARD SUPPLY LIST

Cardstock; crayons (Caran d'Ache)

Masking Tape Background

SIMPLE OFFICE-SUPPLY MASKING TAPE can be transformed into a working surface with just a few strokes of gesso and splashes of watercolor. Applying the tape directly to cardstock and then painting it will create a seamless and unified background. An alternative technique, which I've done here, begins with painting the masking-tape strips on a separate surface. Once the masking tape is painted and has fully dried, the strips can be peeled from the non-porous working surface and applied to the cardstock background of the layout. Rearranging the strips from the order in which they were painted creates a random yet unique and artistic background.

PAGE SUPPLY LIST

Cardstock; gesso (Liquitex); watercolor paint (Winsor & Newton); letter stickers, rub-on accents (Making Memories); buttons (MOD); photo corners (Heidi Swapp); artist crayons (Caran d'Ache)

For this technique, you'll need:

Masking tape

Plastic placemat (or other non-porous surface)

White gesso

Water

Brushes

Watercolor paint

Cardstock

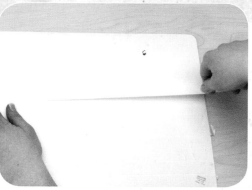

1 APPLY STRIPS OF TAPE

Lay down long strips of masking tape across the top of a plastic placemat (or other non-porous surface). Place the strips as close as possible.

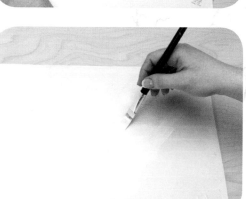

2 ADD GESSO

Randomly brush the taped placemat with white gesso, leaving some areas uncovered. Try dropping watered-down gesso onto the tape and letting the drip marks dry in place. You can let the gesso dry before moving on to Step 3 (which creates a more layered look) or leave the gesso wet to allow the colors to mix.

3 PAINT WITH WATERCOLOR

Splash, brush and drip blue watercolor onto the strips using a brush. The messier you leave the paint, the more textured and varied your finished background will be; even paint coverage will create a uniform background. Once the paint is dry, peel the strips of tape from the placemat.

31

4 TRANSFER THE TAPE TO YOUR PAGE

Adhere the tape to your cardstock, tearing the tape and placing it in random order to break up the brushstrokes. Once the background is covered in tape strips, fold the extra lengths over the edges and secure on the back. Embellish the painted-tape background with rub-ons, buttons and additional horizontal strips of tape painted green.

Batik-Style Painting
with Masking Fluid

LATEX-BASED, REMOVABLE MASKING FLUID applied to surfaces such as watercolor paper and cardstock will, once dry, resist water-based paint such as watercolor and acrylic. You can use the fluid to protect areas of an image that you want to remain bare or unaffected by subsequently applied color, then remove it when you are finished painting.

For this layout, I washed layers of diluted acrylic paint over the page and used masking to protect certain areas. The final product of this mask-and-wash technique is an image with cleanly defined edges but messy, wash-filled areas. The process of layering paint washes imparts a unique effect to the finished piece not achieved through traditional painting techniques.

PAGE SUPPLY LIST

Cardstock; masking fluid (Winsor & Newton); acrylic paint (Curry's, Tri-Art); gesso (Tri-Art); gold leaf (Stewart Superior); stamps (Autumn Leaves, Magnetic Poetry); pen and ink (Sakura, Speedball, Stewart Superior)

For this technique, you'll need:

Cardstock (light-colored)

Pen

Masking fluid

Brushes

Acrylic paint
(yellow, green, yellow-orange, blue, brown, red)

1 DRAW AND APPLY MASKING

Sketch a design onto cardstock. Paint masking fluid onto the areas you wish to leave bare. I dip my brush right into the bottle of masking fluid since it's kind of messy to put on a palette. Allow the masking to dry about 30 minutes.

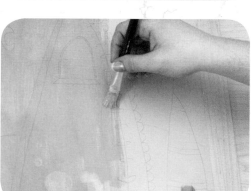

2 PAINT A LAYER OF YELLOW

Add a wash of yellow acrylic paint (watered down) over the entire cardstock. Allow the paint to dry.

3 APPLY MORE MASKING

Paint masking fluid onto the window and outline of the house, plus the dots and lines on the whimsical foliage. Allow the fluid to dry.

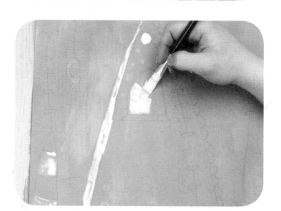

4 APPLY MORE LAYERS OF COLOR AND MASKING

Wash acrylic color over the page again, using darker yellow on the house and the triangular foliage and light green on the background and grass. Hand paint green leaves on the house. Mask vines and leaves and the lines in the grass, plus the dots in edging around the house; wash the background with darker green once the masking is dry. Wash over the house with yellow-orange paint. Mask the grass. Wash over the background sky with blue. Wipe dark brown into some areas of the house; work the paint around with your fingers or a paper towel. Paint one whimsical triangular piece of foliage with red.

Once all the paint is dry, gently rub with your finger to remove the masking.

33

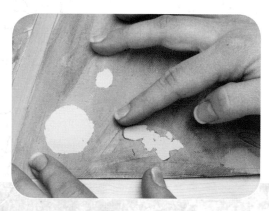

Work from Light to Dark

With this technique, it is important to start with the lightest color of paint and move to the next darkest shade with each subsequent wash, as it is difficult to cover over dark colors with lighter ones.

Frisket Film Mask

FRISKET FILM IS A CLEAR, WATER-RESISTANT, self-adhesive film that can be applied to a variety of surfaces including watercolor paper, cardstock, wood, plastic and metal. Once the film is applied to a painting surface, water-soluble mediums can be added and the area beneath the film mask will be protected from subsequent layers of paint. The film peels off easily once the painting is completed, revealing crisp images.

Frisket film allows the freedom of messy painting while maintaining clean edges. (Although if too many watery layers of paint are applied, some seepage under the edges of the mask may occur.) I like using it to create textured, painterly pieces with crisp edges that would be difficult to achieve without the mask.

PAGE SUPPLY LIST

Cardstock; frisket film (Artool); acrylic paint (Curry's, Tri-Art); watercolor paint (Winsor & Newton); decorative scissors (Fiskars); gesso (Tri-Art); rub-on letters (Autumn Leaves); photo corners (Canson); rhinestones (Westrim); hole punch; floss (DMC); pen

For this technique, you'll need:

Designs printed onto paper

Frisket film

Craft knife

Scissors or decorative-edge scissors (optional)

Permanent marker (optional)

Cardstock

Acrylic paint (yellow, green, crimson)

White gesso

Watercolor paint (blue)

1 DRAW AND CUT

Print mask designs onto paper. Place the paper under the film and cut out the shape with a craft knife, cutting on the paper side of the film instead of the film side. (Cutting on the film side may make the film pull and distort.) Here, I'm cutting a stem and leaf design.

2 CUT MORE SHAPES

You may also draw your design on the paper side of the film with a permanent marker and cut out the design with regular scissors or decorative-edge scissors. Here, I'm cutting out a round flower mask.

3 START PEELING

Partially peel the film away from the paper. »

35

A Word about Acrylics

You can use any kind of acrylic paint for the techniques in this book. I use jar acrylics because they are more pigmented and seem to go farther even though they tend to be more expensive. However, you may use the bottled acrylic paints found in craft stores if you like.

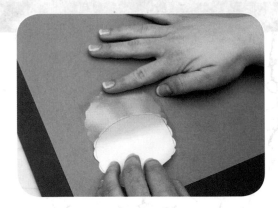

4 PLACE THE MASK

Lay the top of the round flower mask on the surface and slowly peel the paper away as you press the mask in place. To retain some of the cardstock color, trace the round flower mask onto the bottom-left part of the paper and paint the area with yellow acrylic.

5 PAINT AND ADD MORE MASKS

Cover the cardstock with green acrylic, painting right over the masked flower shape. Place more masks onto the background. Here, I am adding a stem and leaves.

6 ADD MORE LAYERS OF PAINT AND FINAL MASKS

Paint a layer of white gesso over the entire paper. Once dry, brush and drop on blue watercolor. Let this layer dry, then apply the last of the masks. Next, apply the final layer of paint (crimson acrylic) over the entire background. Let the paint dry.

7 REMOVE ALL MASKS

Carefully pull up the masks to reveal the finished background. Notice that I have painted each layer of color over the entire background to create a sense of continuity; some seams and edges of the underlayers may be visible in the finished piece if you paint only the area immediately surrounding the mask.

Protect Previously Finished Areas

I cut a piece of frisket film to protect the portion of this layout done in watercolor and ink from the messy background of the rest of the page. The transparent nature of the film made it easy to trace my pre-painted shape. The film allowed me to splash and drip watercolor onto my page without ruining my completed work.

PAGE SUPPLY LIST

Watercolor paint and paper (Winsor & Newton); chipboard stars (Making Memories); stamps (Ma Vinci); brads, sticker accent (Making Memories); buttons (MOD); adhesive foam; pen and ink (Speedball, Stewart Superior)

Watercolor and Ink
Illustration

EVEN IF YOU ARE NOT CONFIDENT in your own drawing abilities, the simplest of designs will look fabulous when illustrated with this method. Absolutely everything seems to look better when hand drawn in ink and filled with watercolor.

As with many other painting techniques, I have found the secret to beautiful watercolor and ink illustrations lies in not overworking the paper or paint too much. Draw with a free, light hand, and apply the paint in delicate washes (layers). Avoid the temptation to rework your piece until it appears perfect; the appeal of your finished piece will be its messy imperfection.

PAGE SUPPLY LIST
Blending medium, watercolor paint and paper (Winsor & Newton); pen, permanent pigmented acrylic ink (Speedball)

1 SKETCH IN PENCIL, THEN INK

Sketch your illustration with pencil on watercolor paper. Then ink the illustration using permanent ink. Here, I used an extra-fine-line nib pen because I like the wobbly, uneven look of the lines it makes. But you can also experiment with a regular permanent-ink pen; find what works for you.

For this technique, you'll need:

Watercolor paper

Pencil

Permanent pigmented acrylic ink (black)

Extra-fine-line nib pen or permanent-ink pen

Watercolor paint

Palette

Round (nos. 3 and 5) and flat (no. 12) brushes

Blending medium

Modeling paste

2 PAINT THE DETAILS

Place watercolor in your palette and paint the detail on the painting. Here, I'm using a no. 3 round brush. I find that with this brush and a no. 5 round brush, I am able to paint all of the details on an image like this.

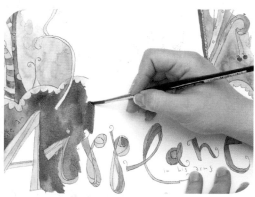

3 PREPARE THE PAINT TO COVER MORE PAPER

Mix blending medium with the watercolors to slow the drying time so that large areas can be painted without visible drying lines.

39

4 FILL IN THE LARGE AREAS

Use the watercolor/blending medium to fill in the large areas of your painting. Fill in large, open areas with a no. 12 flat brush, and continue using a no. 5 round brush to fill in the areas around the letters and other details. To deepen the color, go back over it with additional washes of watercolor.

Modeling Paste

Left in right,
they fit together
hand in hand
and complement each other
well.

she asks; she answers.
she takes; she gives.
she runs; she follows.
our two girls,
sweet each in their own way
they go together
apart and one,

counterbalanced
like night and day.

Valen's Augob

40

FOR A SOFTER EFFECT THAN WATERCOLOR ILLUSTRATION, this technique uses pencil-like etched lines and colored chalks. The toothy finish of modeling paste readily accepts chalk, and you have more control over the colors. Plus, by using chalk on modeling paste you can more readily achieve a brighter look compared with using chalk on paper.

PAGE SUPPLY LIST

Corrugated cardboard; modeling paste (Tri-Art); chalk (Craf-T); metal stylus; twine; fixative spray (Krylon); pen and ink (Speedball)

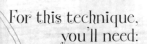

For this technique, you'll need:

Cardboard

Canvas-tinted gesso

Craft stick

Fine-point metal stylus

Colored chalk

Eye makeup applicators

Modeling paste

1 COVER WITH GESSO, THEN PASTE

Cover a piece of cardboard with canvas-tinted gesso. Once dry, smooth modeling paste over the cardboard using a craft stick. The application doesn't need to be even, but it should be smooth. Set it aside to dry.

2 ETCH A DRAWING

Using a fine-point metal stylus, draw a design onto the dried modeling paste. The look of the drawing will be like that of pencil, but the lines won't smudge.

3 ADD COLOR WITH CHALK

Using your finger, rub some colored chalk into the background of the illustration. Then use eye makeup applicators to fill in the design details with chalk.

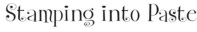

Stamping into Paste

The images on these cards were stamped into wet modeling paste rather than etched with a stylus. A very thin layer of paste works best with stamping to achieve the finest detail. Use a fine-point, stiff-bristled paintbrush to work the chalk thoroughly into the crevices of the impressed image.

CARD SUPPLY LIST

Cardstock; watercolor paper (Winsor & Newton); stamps (Sugarloaf); modeling paste (Tri-Art); chalk (Craf-T)

CHAPTER TWO

Sparkly

Beads and brads, objects on wire, things made from wire, and glitter, glitter everywhere! It's amazing how just a little touch of sparkle can add so much to a page. By the end of this chapter you'll think no project is complete without just a little shimmer and shine!

In WaITInG

they dressed and waited for the guests to arrive, they were ready to party.

Glitter

THOUGH TYPICALLY QUITE MESSY, GLITTER can be applied in a controlled way to accent select areas with a little shine. For example, the simple step of sealing a stamped image on chipboard with matte gel acrylic medium and highlighting the details in fine, powdery glitter finishes the piece and gives it a polished look. Glitter is a great way to take your homemade embellishments to the next level.

44

PAGE SUPPLY LIST

Cardstock; watercolor paint (Winsor & Newton); patterned paper (Chatterbox); glitter (Stix2Anything, other); chipboard letters, journaling spots (Heidi Swapp); stamps (artist's own design, Creative Imaginations); photo corners (Anna Griffin, Canson, Heidi Swapp); clear topcoat (Ranger); rub-on accents (BasicGrey); chalk (Craf-T); sticker accents (Making Memories); decorative scissors (Provo Craft); ink (Stewart Superior); pen (Sakura)

For this technique,
you'll need:

Stamps and ink

White cardstock

Pen (optional)

*Watercolor paint
(optional)*

Chipboard

*Matte gel acrylic
medium or glue stick*

Scissors

Glitter

Transparent microbeads

Small plate

*Dimensional clear
glass medium*

1 PREPARE THE IMAGES

Stamp your images on white cardstock. (I carved my own cake stamps
for this layout.) Add pen outlines
and watercolor to the images if
desired. For items you want to be
dimensional, cut around the cardstock shape, leaving a quarter-inch
(7mm) border on all sides. Adhere
the cardstock to the chipboard with
matte gel or a glue stick. Cut out the
dimensional images from the chipboard; also cut out the flat images.

2 APPLY GLUE AND GLITTER

Place each image on a small plate,
and cover the image with the
dimensional clear gloss medium.
Then sprinkle glitter over it, covering it completely. Set it aside to dry.
Once the adhesive is fully dried, tap
off excess glitter.

3 ADD A TOUCH OF SPARKLE

To simply accent some of the
stamped pieces, make lines or
designs with the dimensional clear
gloss medium. Then sprinkle
microbeads onto the piece, covering it completely. Set it aside to dry.
Once it is dry, tap off excess beads.

Shimmery Paper Accents

he searched two cities wide for the perfect birthday bike, it had to be perfect for her to ride, the colour of cream soda and with pink

streamers too, he found it and knew nothing else would do.

this was the bike. he had to have it.

SPECIALLY TEXTURED PAPERS SUCH AS GLITTER STREAMERS naturally draw the eye because of their sparkle and shimmer, but their delicate nature can make them tricky to use. They are tough to adhere and do not always cut easily into fun shapes. However, with very simple cutting and a little creative application, you can boost a page's pizzazz to the maximum and keep your frustration to a minimum!

PAGE SUPPLY LIST

Cardstock; brads, patterned paper (MOD); glitter paper (unknown); iron-on letters, journaling accents, photo corners (Heidi Swapp); letter stickers (Making Memories); rhinestones (Westrim); glitter (Stix2Anything); pen (Sakura)

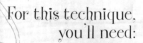

For this technique,
you'll need:

*Thin, sparkly specialty
papers (iridescent,
metallic tissue)*

Cardstock

Scissors

Transparent tape

1 CUT PAPERS INTO STRIPS

Cut pieces of sparkly paper into long, thin strips. I used iridescent paper and metallic tissue paper cut into quater-inch (6mm) to 1-inch (2.5cm) strips.

2 ATTACH TO THE PAGE

Cut a 2-inch (5cm) circle from a sheet of cardstock. Turn the cardstock over and loosely tape on the strips so that they show through the cutout circle.

Match the Method of Application to the Theme

47

To complement the photo's watery background, I crumpled and tossed handfuls of blue and silver glitter paper onto the cardstock and tacked the pieces lightly wherever they touched the page, working gently so as not to disturb the random mess where it had fallen. To carry the "entangled" theme further, I allowed a long piece of twill and some twine to tangle around the title as it wound its way across the page.

PAGE SUPPLY LIST

Cardstock; patterned paper (7gyspies); glitter paper (unknown); twill (Autumn Leaves); twine; chipboard letters (Heidi Swapp); photo corners (American Crafts); floss (DMC); pen and ink (Speedball)

Sequin Sprays

she orbits

adoration like
gravity,
pulls her in,
she orbits, little
satellite,
drawn to the sun.

SEQUINS CAN EASILY BE SEWN OR GLUED ON, but when wrapped around the end of a fine wire, sequins create a delicate ornamental spray that adds great movement and line to the composition of a page. By securing the ends of the wire on the back side of the page, the sequin sprays will stand up off the paper. These sequin sprays could represent delicate flowers, shooting stars or exciting explosions of confetti.

PAGE SUPPLY LIST

Patterned paper (7gypsies, K&Co., MOD); vellum; brads (Making Memories); sequins (Doodlebug, unknown); wire (Westrim); rub-on letters (Mustard Moon); felt; photo corners (Heidi Swapp); gesso (Tri-Art); watercolor paint (Winsor & Newton); chipboard circles (Technique Tuesday); clock accent (Heidi Swapp); glitter (Stix2Anything); pen (Sakura)

1 ATTACH WIRE TO THE SEQUIN

Cut a length of fine-gauge wire. Thread the wire through the hole in the sequin and wrap the wire beneath the hole to secure it.

For this technique, you'll need:

Fine-gauge wire

Sequins

Hole punch

Cardstock

Transparent tape

2 WIRE MORE SEQUINS AND INSERT INTO CARDSTOCK

Repeat with two more sequins. Wrap the ends of the three wires together. Punch a hole in the cardstock and insert the wires from the front of the hole to the back.

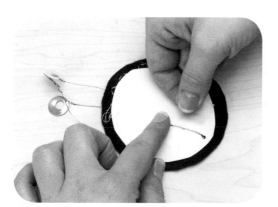

3 SECURE TO THE BACK

Turn the cardstock over and secure the end of the wire with tape.

4 CREATE A SPRAY

For a spray effect, insert the ends of the wire into individual holes and secure all the ends of the wire to the back of the cardstock.

49

Iridescent Medium

FrOsty

she suited this frosty afternoon, both pale and rosy. Summer Lily on a winter day.

IRIDESCENT MEDIUM IS A WATER-BASED, shimmering substance that can be mixed with watercolor to add luster to the paint or applied directly to a working surface for more intense sparkle. Pour it, pool it or paint it: iridescent medium is an artist-quality product that can give your painted pieces shine without cracking, peeling or shedding bits of glitter all over your work. However, take care to wash your brushes and water cup carefully after using iridescent medium, or your next painting will also sparkle when you might not want it to!

PAGE SUPPLY LIST

Iridescent medium, watercolor paint and paper (Winsor & Newton); chipboard letters (Heidi Swapp); photo corners (Canson); snowflakes (American Crafts); rhinestones (Westrim); pen and ink (Speedball)

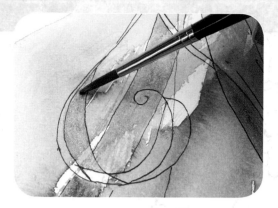

For this technique,
you'll need:

Watercolor paper

Watercolor paint
(various shades of pink)

Brushes

White gouache
(opaque watercolor)

Pencil

Pen and black
waterproof ink

Iridescent medium
for watercolor

Chipboard letters
(light-colored, finished)

Gesso (if using unfinished
chipboard letters)

VARY THE COLOR AND THE AMOUNT OF MEDIUM

Wash a 9-inch (30cm) square of watercolor paper with medium pink paint. (It is not necessary to tape down the paper for this technique.) Lightly sketch swirls in pencil once the paint is dry; outline in black waterproof ink. (See page 38 for more information on this technique.)

Add a drop of iridescent medium to shades of pink watercolor and white gouache, and mix it in using an old brush. Paint the swirls in shades of pink, varying the paint color and amount of iridescent medium. Allow the paint to dry.

PAINT LETTERS WITH PIZZAZZ

Lightly sand finished chipboard letters (or paint with white gesso if unfinished, then sand lightly). Paint the letters using just the iridescent medium to create a sparkly title.

51

Pour a Puddle onto the Page

For this tag I poured a puddle of iridescent medium directly onto the paper and laid it flat to dry. The effect is a lustrous splatter that dries beautifully, with no cracks or peeling. Dilute the medium with a little water or watercolor for a less intense effect.

PAGE SUPPLY LIST

Iridescent medium, watercolor paint and paper (Winsor & Newton); chipboard; matte gel (Tri-Art); button (Autumn Leaves); ribbon (Li'l Davis)

Metal Foil Tape

The Machine 197

they hoisted that baby up there and

tinkered on it all day

I ADMIRE THE LOOK OF RUSTED METAL, but unfortunately an entire background of heavy metal is just not suitable for scrapbooks. However, the look can be reproduced with metal foil tape and acrylic paint. This tape—found in hardware stores, and traditionally used for repairing heating ducts—has the same weight and feel of aluminum foil, and it is an inexpensive and easy way to achieve the look of heavy metal on your layouts without the bulk and weight. Distressing the tape by crumpling and then smoothing it out again gives it the look of a junkyard find, while faux aging techniques give the page a nice patina.

PAGE SUPPLY LIST

Cardstock; metal foil tape, hardware, photo corners (unknown); metal frames (Nunn Designs); acrylic paint (Rheotech)

For this technique, you'll need:

Metal foil tape

Cardstock

Acrylic paint
(red oxide, raw umber)

Paper towel

1 TEAR AND PLACE THE TAPE

Rip pieces of metal foil tape, crumple them a little in your hand, remove the backing and place them randomly on a sheet of cardstock. Overlap some of the pieces and run them in different directions.

2 ADD A LAYER OF RED

With your fingers, wipe a thin layer of red oxide acrylic paint over the tape, working it into the grooves of the tape. The layer doesn't need to be even; it actually looks better if it's not.

3 WIPE AWAY SOME PAINT

Let the paint dry for a few minutes, then rub away some of the paint with a paper towel. Allow the remaining paint to finish drying.

4 ADD AND REMOVE MORE PAINT

With your fingers, apply a thin, uneven layer of raw umber acrylic paint, again working paint into grooves of the tape. Let this dry for a few minutes, then rub away some of the paint with a paper towel.

53

Why Not Just Use Aluminum Foil?

The advantage of metal foil tape is that it is self-adhesive and paper-backed, making the tape simple to tear off, crumple, pierce, stitch or otherwise distress it and then stick it on a page.

Gold Leaf

In WAITING

they dressed and waited for the guests to arrive, they were ready to party.

GOLD LEAF IS A THIN SHEET, or leaf, of gold that can be adhered to a variety of surfaces, including paper and home décor items, using a special water-soluble liquid adhesive called *gold size*. Gold or silver leaf is available in both artificial and authentic metals. Artificial gold is thicker and can be handled with your fingertips; however, authentic gold should be lifted into place using a brush to prevent the gold from sticking to your fingers. Typically, real gold leaf is applied using a soft-bristled brush called a gilder's tip, though I find the stiff-bristled brushes I have on hand work just a well. To protect your work from tarnishing, finish it with sealers made specially for metal leafing applications.

PAGE SUPPLY LIST

Cardstock; gold size (unknown); gold leaf (Stewart Superior); watercolor paint (Winsor & Newton); letters (K&Co.); chipboard circles (Bazzill, Technique Tuesday); pen (Sakura)

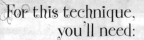

For this technique, you'll need:

Cardstock (cut into a shape, if desired)

Gold size (water-soluble liquid adhesive)

Small round brush and additional brushes

Gold leaf

Gilder's tip (optional)

1 PLAN AND APPLY SIZE TO THE SHAPES

Draw the shapes intended for leafing onto cardstock (mine is crown-shaped) with a pencil. Here I drew a series of leaves and stems. Avoid too much fine detail in your design. Using a small brush, apply gold size to the areas intended for leafing, then wash the brush immediately. Let the size dry according to the manufacturer's directions.

2 APPLY THE GOLD

If using artificial gold, use your fingertip to apply small pieces of gold leaf to dried adhesive. Alternatively, use a gilder's tip brush or any other brush to apply real gold leaf. Gently rub the leaf with your fingertip (or brush) to adhere.

3 REMOVE THE EXCESS

Once the image is covered with leaf, remove the excess using your fingertip or brush. Then brush excess leaf from the image.

55

A Little Gold Goes a Long Way

Be sure to consider the size of a project when you're applying gold leaf so as not to overwhelm the design. Just a touch of gold leaf adds the perfect highlight of color on this floral card.

PROJECT SUPPLY LIST

Watercolor paint and paper (Winsor & Newton); photo corners (Canson); gold leaf (Stewart Superior); pen and ink (Speedball)

Eyelets

I LOVE FINDING NEW WAYS TO USE OLD THINGS, and this technique does just that. The process involves setting lots of eyelets into cardstock and painting over the entire piece using acrylic paint. The color of eyelets doesn't matter, so this is a good opportunity to use up those mismatched or outdated colors. The apparent weight and heavy texture of the metal rings coupled with the airy look provided by the eyelet holes make eyelets intriguing additions to your pages.

PAGE SUPPLY LIST

Cardstock; eyelets (Doodlebug, Making Memories); paint (Rheotech, Venetian); gloss medium (Tri-Art); letter accents (K&Co., Autumn Leaves); decorative scissors (Provo Craft); conchos (Scrapworks); pen (Sakura)

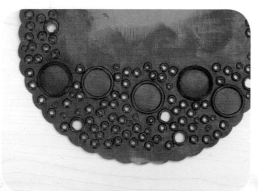

For this technique,
you'll need:

Cardstock

Scissors

Anywhere hole punch

Hammer

Round eyelets (large and
small, in any color)

Eyelet setting tool

Acrylic paint

Brush

Conchos
(large and small)

Gloss medium (optional)

1 PUNCH APPROPRIATELY SIZED HOLES

Cut a piece of cardstock to the desired shape. Use an anywhere punch and hammer to punch holes in the cardstock. Make sure the holes are the right size for your eyelets, and space them apart to leave room for the eyelets.

2 SET ALL THE EYELETS

Place the eyelets into the holes and set with the eyelet setting tool and hammer.

3 ADD ACRYLIC PAINT

Use acrylic paint to paint over the entire piece. Let this dry, then apply a second coat of paint to get thorough coverage on the eyelets.

4 EMBELLISH FURTHER

Try using different-sized conchos on the cardstock, too, painting over them just as you did the eyelets. If you like, seal the piece with a gloss medium for a shiny coat.

57

Wire Decorations

MAKING DECORATIVE ELEMENTS OUT OF MALLEABLE METAL is as easy as twisting, turning, pinching and pulling until you're satisfied. Use a pair of needle-nose pliers to grip the wire and create tight turns and bends. Wrap large designs to frame a photo or create smaller pieces to accent a page. I enjoy the rustic look of unfinished wire, but a few seconds with a can of spray paint can transform the wire to match any color on your layout.

PAGE SUPPLY LIST

Cardstock; watercolor paint and paper (Winsor & Newton); gesso (Tri-Art); letter stickers (Making Memories); artist's crayons (Caran d'Ache); metal charm (Westrim); wire; pen and ink (Speedball)

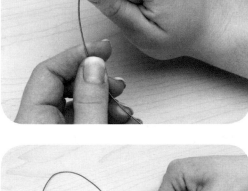

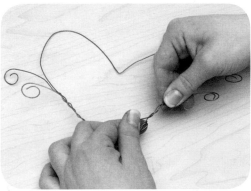

For this technique, you'll need:

6 feet (1.3m) of 18-gauge galvanized wire

Needle-nose pliers

Wire cutters

1 BEGIN THE HEART WITH A BEND

Cut one piece of wire to 20 inches (50cm). Use needle-nose pliers to bend the wire to make a heart.

2 FINISH THE HEART AND CREATE CURLS

Finish the heart by twisting the wire ends to form a large loop of wire. Cut four pieces of wire to about 6 inches (15cm) long. Use the pliers to create a curl at the end of each length of wire.

3 TWIST THE CURLS ONTO THE HEART

Attach the curled wire to the heart by tightly twisting the ends to hold them in place.

4 WRAP THE WIRE

Cut another piece of wire to 18-24 inches (40-60cm) long. Hold the bottom of the heart with pliers and randomly wrap the wire around the bottom of the heart. Secure the end of the wire by wrapping it around the edge of the heart, pinching it tight with the pliers.

59

Beaded Wire

THIN JEWELRY-MAKING WIRE is a perfect frame for beading. Small beads slip easily onto the wire, and the wire holds the form of whatever shape into which you bend it. Using the technique outlined here to form a fancy cobweb, you could also bead wire flowers, hearts, frames or any other shape that you can imagine—and have the time and patience to put together!

PAGE SUPPLY LIST

Cardstock; heavy gauge wire; jewelry making wire; seed beads (Blue Moon); gesso (Tri-Art); iridescent medium, masking fluid, watercolor paint (Winsor & Newton); rub-ons (BasicGrey); felt, star sequins (unknown); floss (DMC); rhinestones (Westrim); photo corners (Canson); pen and ink (Speedball)

1 BUILD THE BASE

Cut one length of wire to 10.5 inches (26cm) and another piece to 5.75 inches (14.5cm). Using needle-nose pliers, twist one end of the short wire at the midpoint of the longer piece to create a squat letter "T" form.

2 STRING AND SECURE

Cut a piece of jewelry wire to 5 inches (12.5cm). Twist one end around the long heavy-gauge wire approximately 1.5 inches (4cm) from the midpoint. String a random assortment of seed beads along the wire to the midpoint of the length. Twist the half-beaded wire around the short heavy-gauge wire 1.5 inches (4cm) from the top, wrapping around once and pulling tight to secure.

3 FILL IN THE WEB

Continue beading the remaining half of the wire and secure the end on the long heavy-gauge wire 1.5 inches (4cm) from the midpoint on the opposite side. This beaded wire should form a semicircle between the two intersecting heavy-gauge wires, forming the first of the three layers of the web. Cut 9.5-inch (24cm) and 13-inch (33cm) lengths of jewelry-making wire; bead and secure two more semicircles around the web, spacing approximately 1.5 inches (4cm) apart.

Next, begin adding the beaded spokes of the web. Cut three 6-inch (15cm) pieces of jewelry-making wire. Twist one piece onto the center point of the web and string it with long beads and a few seed beads for interest. When the spoke has been beaded to the intersection of the first semicircle, wrap the wire around the intersecting semicircle. Continue beading each spoke until the web is complete.

For this technique, you'll need:

Wire cutters

Needle-nose pliers

17 inches (36cm) of heavy-gauge wire

4 feet (1.2m) of jewelry-making wire

Seed beads (mauve, dark purple, clear)

Long beads (clear, light purple)

Shaker Box

she swam in

Like it was the ocean.

FILLED WITH GLITTER, SEQUINS, MINI-BEADS and paper shapes, shaker boxes make fun interactive elements on your page. Size them as large or small as you like, and customize them to your heart's content by changing their contents.

PAGE SUPPLY LIST

Cardstock; paper (FiberMark); transparency; cellophane; rub-on letters (KI Memories); sequins (Doodlebug, other); beads; photo corners (Canson); wire; jump rings (Making Memories); gesso (Tri-Art); watercolor paint (Winsor & Newton); marker (Marvy); pen and ink (Speedball)

1 START THE TRANSPARENT POCKET

To make a full-page shaker box, begin by cutting circles of various sizes from a piece of blue cellophane. Then layer the cellophane over a blank transparency sheet and zigzag stitch around the edges of the sheet and the circles.

2 FORM AND FILL THE POCKET

Place green cardstock behind the stitched window. Stitch the cardstock to three of the window edges, leaving the bottom open. Fill the resulting pocket with water-inspired items: bubble-like sequins and beads and specialty paper handcut into seaweed shapes. Stitch the pocket closed.

3 MAKE A SECOND LAYER

Cut a window from the center of the yellow cardstock to fit a transparency sheet with a quarter-inch (6mm) overlap. Place the transparency behind the cardstock and temporarily adhere the two with transparent tape. Then stitch the transparency to the cardstock.

4 COMBINE THE LAYERS

Cut two fish from specialty paper and thread each with two jump rings. Secure two lengths of white wire to the back of the cardstock window, only adhering the wire on one end. Feed the wire through the jump rings. Secure the wire on the other side of the window.

Using adhesive foam, adhere the two pieces of cardstock (yellow over green), making sure to line them up.

For this technique,
you'll need:

Blue cellophane

Scissors

Two blank
transparency sheets

Sewing machine

Two sheets of cardstock
(green, yellow)

Assorted sequins
and beads

Specialty papers
(for making fish
and seaweed)

Transparent tape

White wire

Four medium-sized
jump rings

Double-sided
foam adhesive

63

CHAPTER THREE

TOUCHY-Feely

A few lengths of ribbon, some scraps of fabric, and basic stitches easily transform layouts into works of textile art. No previous experience necessary! Get your needle and thread, ribbon and fabric, embroidery floss and fibers, and let's get stitching.

she wears her day
like a halo
around her,
around her
things are bright
and they start to glow,
grow real bright,
hot like white
she's phosphorescent,
incandescent,
and everything about her is
just so light,
she's so light,
she's light-hearted
and in her light steps
dancing through her day
lights my day,
she wears her heart,
splendid nimbus,
luminescent,
iridescent,
for all to see;
oh how it shines,
blazing gently.

Ribbon Tabs

THIS WONDERFULLY EASY TECHNIQUE IS A FANTASTIC WAY to use up the mountains of ribbon we all accumulate. On these layouts, each tab is a two-inch (5cm) length of ribbon folded over and secured at the ends, then glued onto the layout. Try a ribbon-tab border for a photo, embellish a single edge of a page or element, or layer color-coordinated tabs on an entire background.

PAGE SUPPLY LIST

Cardstock; ribbon (Heidi Grace, Making Memories, Wrights); photo corners (Heidi Swapp); die-cut strips, flocked paper, tags (Heidi Grace); pen and ink (Speedball); Haettenscheweiler font (Internet download)

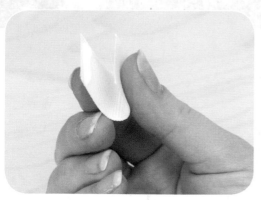

1 CREATE THE TABS

Cut ribbon of various widths into 2-inch (5cm) lengths. Apply a small amount of liquid glue to one end; fold over and press to form a loop. Let the ribbon tabs dry.

For this technique, you'll need:

Ribbon in varying widths

Scissors

Liquid glue

2 PLACE AND GLUE THE TABS

Layer the tabs on the page, starting at the bottom. Lay a thin line of glue on the page and line the tabs side by side. Work your way to the top, placing the next row of ribbon tabs so that the top row covers the unfinished edges of the row beneath.

Try Multi-Textured Tabs

I started this project by laying my photo on a piece of corrugated cardboard, and then began tucking tabs made from anything I could find—paper, mesh, ribbon, twill, lace. I continued until the page seemed full.

PAGE SUPPLY LIST

Cardstock; patterned paper (7gypsies); ribbon (Li'l Davis, May Arts, Wrights, unknown); mesh (Magic Mesh); twill (Autumn Leaves); metal charm (Pebbles); ribbon slides (Maya Road); clips, fabric (unknown); corrugated cardboard; vellum; brush marker (Marvy); pen (Sakura)

Weaving Ribbon
and Paper Strips

Within the layout:
- watches the car go.
- more kisses.
- waves good-bye, again.
- Listens to the sound of the engine.
- Waits till it's gone.
- One last look
- starts the day.

68

WEAVING IS SUCH A VERSATILE TECHNIQUE. A simple change to the style or color of the ribbon or paper strips, and a woven background can easily be adapted for any theme, from the arrival of a new baby to celebrating Christmas. Weaving need not be extensive to be effective; in fact, with just a few glue dots to hold down the ends, you can easily lift and shift the strips in a fun, freestyle pattern.

PAGE SUPPLY LIST

Cardstock; patterned paper (Anna Griffin, KI Memories); photo corners (Canson, Heidi Swapp); ribbon (American Crafts, May Arts, My Mind's Eye); twill (Maya Road); rickrack (Wrights); buttons (Autumn Leaves); pen (Sakura); French Script, Script MT Bold fonts (Internet download)

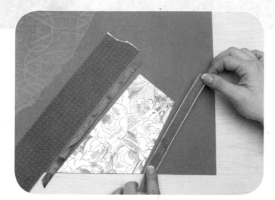

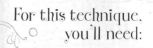

For this technique, you'll need:

Cardstock
(dark orange)

Patterned paper of
various types

Ribbon, twill
and rickrack

Scissors

Glue dots

1 CUT AND PLACE THE STRIPS

Cut strips of patterned paper and ribbon. Vary the lengths of each, from 2 to 10 inches (5cm to 25cm). Glue the piece on which the journaling will be placed onto the background cardstock. Lay paper and ribbon side by side, leaving a gap between each strip, tacking them only at the bottom of the layout with glue dots.

2 BUILD A PATTERN AND SECURE TO THE PAGE

Alternate the direction of the remaining pieces of ribbon, placing them over the layer created in Step 1. Tack down two or three ribbons on the left side. Weave these ribbons above and below the vertical paper and ribbons as desired. No need to keep a strict pattern with the weaving; just do what you like.

Once you are satisfied with your pattern, lift each strip at the ends and secure them in place with glue dots. Trim the ends of the patterned paper around the page and secure the ribbon ends behind the page.

69

Fill up Your Page

This textile-filled page shows how too much is just enough. Feel free to weave layer upon layer of ribbon, twill and paper as I did here. Layer strips, along with a title and other embellishments, in the same direction to unify the design.

PAGE SUPPLY LIST

Cardstock; ribbon (Prima); letter accents (Mustard Moon); tags, twill (Autumn Leaves); fabric (unknown); photo corners and turns (American Crafts); brads (Making Memories); pen and ink (Speedball)

No-Sew
Fabric Additions

If the thought of reaching for a needle and thread or dragging out your sewing machine has you avoiding fabric in your layouts, then try these three easy no-sew techniques. They also enable you to enhance fabric with stamping and other techniques without the risk of breaking down the material.

PAGE SUPPLY LIST

Matte gel (Tri-Art); adhesive denim (DMD); ink (Stewart Superior); stamps (Leave Memories, Ma Vinci); walnut ink (FiberScraps); floss (DMC); photo corners (Canson); fabrics (unknown); pen and ink (Speedball)

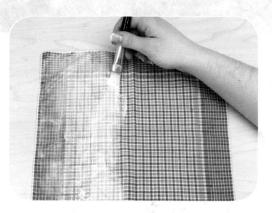

1 BRUSH HANDKERCHIEF WITH MATTE GEL

Brush one side of a handkerchief (I used a vintage hankerchief) with matte gel, then let it dry. This will stiffen the fabric enough to make a stable support for your page. The gel also creates a textured surface that, once dry, allows you to stamp or write on the finished fabric.

2 REINFORCE WITH FREEZER PAPER

Backing calicos and other woven fabrics prone to unraveling with freezer paper provides enough stability to prevent fraying. To do this, iron freezer paper to the back of the material. Set the iron on medium heat and gently press. Then cut the desired shapes from the fabric. Leave the paper backing in place for stiff pieces or remove it immediately before adding to your project.

3 PREPARE DENIM WITH GESSO

Homemade fabric embellishments are a snap using self-adhesive denim. First, brush over the denim with white gesso and allow it to dry.

4 STAMP, WRITE OR DISTRESS

Now the surface is ready to accept stamping or writing. Try stamping over the gesso with solvent ink, and distressing the fabric with walnut ink. This particular ink comes with a dauber, but you can also apply the ink with a spray bottle or other applicator.

Stitching
Torn Paper Strips

are your toes tasty,
do they taste sweet?
oh why do you nibble
upon your baby feet?

TOES
TASTY TASTY

A TORN EDGE OF PAPER LENDS A CAREFREE AIR TO THE ENTIRE PAGE—not to mention there is something incredibly therapeutic about tearing long strips of paper! A neat margin of machine-stitching along a torn edge seems to stabilize the page, as if the stitches are containing the jagged edges.

PAGE SUPPLY LIST

Cardstock; patterned paper (Making Memories, Rhonna Designs); letter stickers (Scrapworks); fabric tape (7gypsies); labels (Li'l Davis, Making Memories); acetate tag (Heidi Swapp); photo corners (Canson); clip (Making Memories); Impact font (Microsoft)

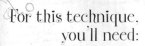
For this technique,
you'll need:

*8.5" x 11" (21.5cm x 28cm)
cardstock (dark brown)*

*Five strips of patterned
paper, cut into 12" x 5"
(30.5cm x 13cm) pieces
(pinks and purples)*

Glue stick

Sewing machine

1 COVER AND STITCH THE PAPER IN PLACE

Starting on the right side of the page, lay a patterned paper strip at a slight angle over the cardstock and use a glue stick to tack it down lightly. Stitch along the right side of the patterned paper strip, leaving a quarter-inch to half-inch (6mm to 13mm) margin to the right of the stitched seam. Continue overlapping strips of paper one at a time until your cardstock is covered.

2 TEAR THE PAPER

Gently tear down the quarter-inch to half-inch (7mm to 13mm) margin of paper, while securing the stitching in place with your other hand.

Layer Surprises   73

Try tucking surprise elements between paper layers. Here, a border of flower petals peaks out just under the photo.

PAGE SUPPLY LIST

*Cardstock (Bazzil); patterned paper
(Chatterbox, K&Co., Rhonna Designs);
flowers (Prima); iron-on letters (Heidi
Swapp); rub-ons (K&Co.); fuzzy rub-ons
(Heidi Swapp); chipboard (unknown); photo
corners (Making Memories); pen and ink
(Speedball); scallop scissors (Provo Craft)*

Machine-Stitched
Shapes

Saved all their money and wrapped it carefully, placed under the tree. Woke Christmas morning as if Santa left it there.

the Christmas TRRaiN

1957

As a child I loved the smooth satiny finish of embroidered appliqué shapes and found the small, detailed stitches fascinating. Employing a sewing machine to stitch and fill in an area on your layout provides a satisfactory substitute for intricate appliqué. To create this look, use a small needle and small stitch length to fill a shape, stitching over it again to complete any missing areas.

PAGE SUPPLY LIST

Cardstock; chipboard letters (Autumn Leaves, Scenic Route); gesso (Tri-Art); stamp (Sugarloaf); silver leaf, stamping ink (Stewart Superior); brads (Making Memories); glitter (Stix2Anything); buttons (Autumn Leaves); metal frame (Nunn Design); sequin (Doodlebug); photo corners (Heidi Swapp); postage stamp frames (Maya Road); acetate star (American Crafts); handmade papers, mylar, snowflake sequin (unknown); floss (DMC); artist's crayons (Caran d'Ache); pen and ink (Speedball)

For this technique,
you'll need:

Cardstock

Thread

Sewing machine

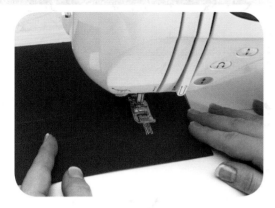

1 **SKETCH AND START
STITCHING**

Sketch the desired shape onto cardstock. Using a sewing machine, first
stitch forward across the shape.

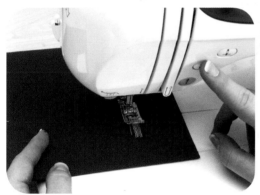

2 **FILL IN THE SHAPE**

Now stitch backward across the shape.
Continue this forward-and-backward
stitching process for the entire shape.

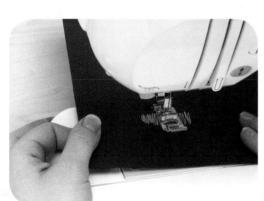

3 **GO OVER IT AGAIN**

Stitch over the entire shape, backward and
forward, a second time to thicken and fill it
in more completely.

Stitch Support

*I have never found cardstock backing to
perforate or fall apart while stitching. But if you are
going to stitch on thinner paper, first back it with
fusible webbing intended for embroidery on fabric for
additional support.*

Embroidery

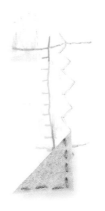

EMBROIDERY MAKES SUCH A UNIQUE ADDITION to a scrapbook, and is yet another technique that when broken down into a few simple steps is easy enough for anyone to try. The stitching for the project shown on this page was created using a standard running stitch and three basic stitches: the feather stitch, the French knot and the chain stitch.

PAGE SUPPLY LIST

Cardstock; muslin; floss (DMC); needle; threads; felt (American Crafts); Helvetica font (Microsoft)

STITCH LAYERS OF FABRIC

Stitch together several layers of fabric (I used muslin) to create a thick, stable background for embroidery. Then choose from the stitches below to create your design.

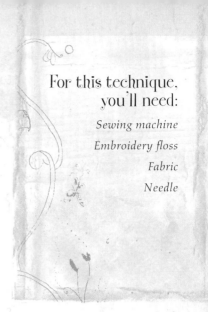
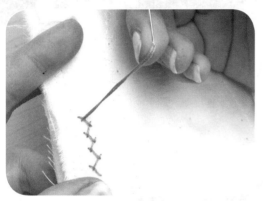

FEATHER STITCH

This off-set zigzag stitch makes great stems or vines, or can finish a seam with visual interest. To create it, make an angled stitch, bringing the needle up and and back down through the fabric. Then bring the needle up beside the angled stitch and make a small stitch perpendicular to the first.

1 FRENCH KNOT, PART ONE

Pull a needle threaded with three strands of embroidery floss through the fabric. Wrap the floss three times around the needle.

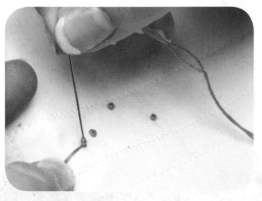

2 FRENCH KNOT, PART TWO

Push the needle through the fabric very near the spot where it was pulled from the back. To make more knots, push the needle back through to the front and repeat. After the last knot, tie off the thread on the back of the fabric. »

77

Sew and Go

Embroidery projects can be time consuming, but their light weight and ease of transport make them easy to carry with you and complete on the go. A few stolen moments during long waits at the doctor's office, during ballet practices or on car rides can quickly add up to a finished project.

1 CHAIN STITCH, PART ONE

Use the chain stitch to create flower petals and stems for your page. To begin, bring the needle from the back to the front of the fabric and then push it back through the same hole (Point A) without pulling the thread all the way through. This will create a loop of floss.

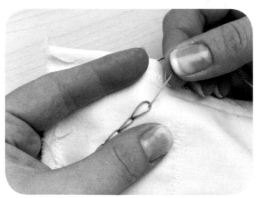

2 CHAIN STITCH, PART TWO

Next, bring the needle up through the fabric above Point A and pass the needle through the loop. Gently pull the floss from the front side of the fabric to pull the loop closed. Continue to make chains. For the last loop in a chain, push the needle through the fabric on the outside of the loop and tie off in the back.

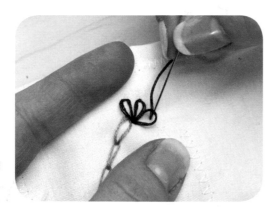

3 CHAIN STITCH, PART THREE

Using a new color of floss, make three separate chain stitches side by side to create a flower. Begin each loop of floss at the same point.

she calls her on the phone and tells her about the day. She trusts her with secrets, and she listens to her when she says everything will be okay. She is the place she turns to when things seem unwell,
where she feels safe.
summer LiLy and gung. 04.06

Alternative to Multiple Layers of Fabric

For this page, I stiffened the muslin with a quick coat of gesso first, rather than stitching several layers together. A few strokes of watercolor across the piece once I completed the embroidery added an extra touch of color.

PAGE SUPPLY LIST

Muslin; gesso (Tri-Art); watercolor paint (Winsor & Newton); chipboard letters (Heidi Swapp); buttons (Autumn Leaves); decorative pin (Heidi Grace); floss (DMC); pen and ink (Speedball)

Couching Stitch

DISCOVERING COUCHING—a loose stitch used to tack down ribbons, yarn and other bulky textiles—will give you a new way to use fibers on your page. With this technique, the usually challenging nature of fluffy or floppy threads actually becomes a plus.

PAGE SUPPLY LIST

Cardstock; patterned paper (BasicGrey); mylar (unknown); fibers (Maya Road); ribbon (Li'l Davis); brad (MOD); rub-on accents, tag (7gypsies); label (Making Memories); pen (Sakura)

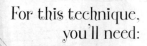
1 PENCIL THE DESIGN AND PUNCH HOLES

With a pencil, draw the design that the fiber will follow. Place the cardstock (or paper) on a soft surface and poke holes in the design every half-inch to three-quarters-inch (13mm to 19mm) using a large needle.

2 TRAP THE THREADS

Knot a thread and pull it up from the back of the paper to the front through one of the holes. Lay the fibers in place, then trap the fibers with the thread by going back down through the same hole that you went up.

3 FORM FLOWER PETALS

To create a flower, poke two holes about a quarter-inch (6mm) apart near the end of the stem. Bring the needle up to the front, create a loop with the fibers to form a petal, and trap the petal end with the thread by going down through the same hole. To form a second petal, go up through the second hole and repeat.

4 ADD A CENTER

Create three more petals in the same way, alternating between the two holes. Then, form a small loop of a contrasting color fiber for the center. Using one of the two holes, pull the thread tight around the loop and tie a knot in the thread at the back of the layout to secure. Trim the ends of the fiber to finish.

81

Hand-Stitched
Badge

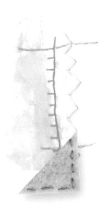

As a child I loved badges—those little stitched awards I received for such accomplishments as completing a swimming course or learning a new task with my Brownie troop. At the end of my daughter Summer Lily's first year of swimming lessons, I was aghast to learn that the little embroidered badges of my youth had been replaced by dull-looking stickers created from photocopies. I decided to try my hand at embroidering my own swimming badges, and the result was homemade embellishments themed to record that first year of swimming.

PAGE SUPPLY LIST

Cardstock; patterned paper (Chatterbox, KI Memories); chipboard letters, photo corners (Heidi Swapp); gesso (Liquitex); decorative scissors (Provo Craft); floss (DMC); thread; muslin; bubble wrap; sandpaper; ink (Winsor & Newton); pen (Speedball)

82

For this technique, you'll need:

Muslin or other plain, flat fabric

Scissors

Pencil or thin marker

Embroidery floss

Small needle

Cardstock

Glue stick

1 CUT AND SKETCH

Cut muslin to the desired shape, leaving about a half-inch (1cm) border around what will be the finished badge size. Lightly draw an image (here, a bikini) in pencil or thin marker on the muslin.

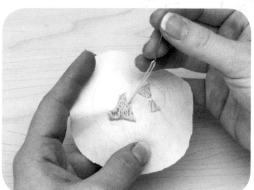

2 FILL IN THE SOLID AREAS

Thread a needle with three strands of embroidery floss and begin to fill in solid areas of the image. Use short stitches laid closely together so there will be no gaps with muslin showing through.

3 STITCH OUTLINES, DETAILS AND WORDS

With a single strand of dark brown embroidery floss, outline the image using short stitches. (Stitches that are too long will create a jagged outline.) The closer the stitches are, the smoother the outline will be. Use this same thread and stitch to write text on the badge.

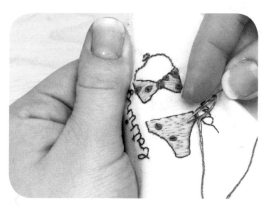

With orange thread and short stitches, add straps to the bikini. Use French knots (see page 77) for the polka dots. After the last knot, tie off the thread on the back of the badge.

4 FINISH THE BADGE

Cut a second piece of muslin the same size as the muslin you are embroidering. Cut a piece of cardstock to the size of the finished badge Place the badge face down. Lay the second piece of muslin on top of that and cardstock circle on top. Fold the muslin over the cardstock, pulling it taut, and secure to the cardstock with a glue stick. Finish by sewing a blanket stitch around the edges of the folded fabric. To make a blanket stitch, push the thread to the front of the fabric and make a small stitch without pulling the stitch tight. Then push the needle from the back through the loop and pull tight.

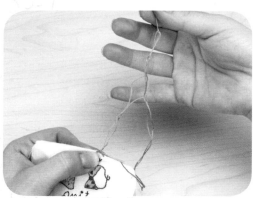

Crazy Quilting

I LOVE CRAZY QUILTING—IT REQUIRES NO EXACT MEASUREMENTS or precise cuts. And as my work table quickly piled up with snippets of ribbon, I found a way to incorporate my love of crazy quilts into a simple project for my scrapbooks: embellishments made from ribbon scraps! Some felt backing, short pieces of ribbon and a few simple embroidery stitches are all that you need to complete crazy quilt pieces such as these simple hearts.

PAGE SUPPLY LIST

Cardstock; patterned paper (Autumn Leaves); tags (Heidi Grace); letter stickers (Heidi Swapp); photo corners (BasicGrey, Canson, Heidi Swapp); journaling stickers (7gypsies); flower (Prima); ribbon (Li'l Davis, Making Memories, Wrights); thread; pen (Sakura)

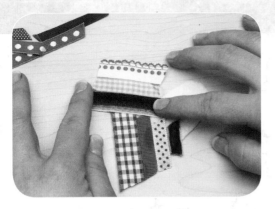

For this technique, you'll need:

Felt (cut into a heart shape)
Assorted ribbon
Glue stick
Embroidery floss
Needle

1 APPLY RIBBON

Use a glue stick to randomly apply short lengths of ribbon to the felt heart, leaving no spaces between the ribbons. Make sure to cut ribbon lengths long enough to hang over the edge of the heart.

2 ADD VARIOUS STITCHES

Use embroidery floss to apply a variety of decorative stitches to fill in the seams between adjacent ribbons.

3 FINISH THE EDGE

Fold the raw ribbon edges to the back side of the felt. Sew a blanket stitch (see page 83) around the edges of the heart to finish the quilt.

85

Sewn Mini-Album

SEWING CAN BE PURELY DECORATIVE but it can also be functional. In this mini-album comprised of delightfully delicate materials, both lightweight and transparent, all the materials are held together with stitching. Even the album is bound together with loose stitches run through clear buttons. The album pages are made from one package of white tissue paper, first sewn together and then embellished.

MINI-ALBUM SUPPLY LIST

Tissue paper; printed acetate (Rhonna Designs); lace; fabrics; wireless chenille (Westrim); sequins (Doodlebug, unknown); ribbon (May Arts, unknown); gesso (Liquitex); watercolor paint (Winsor & Newton); clip, labels (Making Memories); paper flowers (Doodlebug); buttons (Autumn Leaves); photo corners (Canson); floss (DMC); acetate tags and tabs (Heidi Grace); acetate photo corners, felt tags (American Crafts); vellum (Anna Griffin, Canson, DMD); rub-on accents (BasicGrey); pen and ink (Speedball)

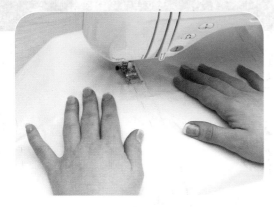

1 PREPARE THE PAGES

Unfold a package of tissue paper. Measure 6.5-inch (16.5cm) panels across the short width of the paper, leaving approximately one inch (2.5cm) between each panel. Sew a straight stitch on the lines on each side of the 1-inch (2.5cm) panels.

2 CUT THE PAGES

Using a ruler and a craft knife, cut the panels apart by cutting down the center of the 1-inch (2.5cm) panels, between the sewn lines. Next, cut the pages of your book apart by cutting the long panels into 6.5-inch (16.5cm) squares. »

For this technique, you'll need:

One package (20 sheets) of tissue paper

Sewing machine

Embroidery floss

Ruler

Craft knife

Scissors

Lightweight fabrics (like tulle, taffeta and printed cottons)

Binding material (like lace, mesh, ribbon, silk flowers)

Glue stick

Additional materials (like wireless chenille)

8 large buttons

Needle

3 EMBELLISH THE EDGES

Sew binding material to the side of each page using items like fabric, ribbon, lace and mesh. For one of my pages, I cut a silk flower into quarters, tacked them onto the edge of the page with a glue stick and sewed them onto the edge of the page. For the satin blanket binding, I cut tabs of ribbon, tucked the cut ends between the layers of tissue paper and stitched the edge of the page.

4 CREATE A VARIETY OF PAGES

Add other types of pages to the album, like this one that is a piece of tulle on which I've embroidered a rectangle using three strands of embroidery floss. Along the edges, I sewed on wireless chenille using a loose zigzag stitch on my sewing machine.

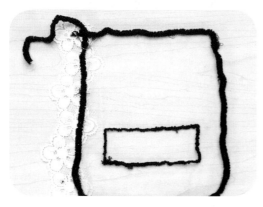

5 BEGIN BINDING THE BOOK

Gather up all the pages with the binding strips on the same side. On the album cover, place a large button at the top. Thread a needle and pass it through one of the button holes to the back of the album.

6 FINISH THE BINDING

Place a second button on the back of the book, and push the needle down through one hole of this button and back up through another hole, passing the needle all the way through to the front of the book.

Push the needle through the second hole of the top button. Tie the two ends of the thread together to secure the pages together. Repeat for additional buttons.

Add Embellishments to the Album

Use techniques and add embellishments that echo the delicate, handmade
look of the album pages. I stitched torn tags with handwritten captions into
place using a single strand of embroidery floss. A window with hand-cut
edges gives a sneak-peak of a page to come. And loose binding allows the
seams between the pages (here, ribbon tabs and silk flowers) to show through.

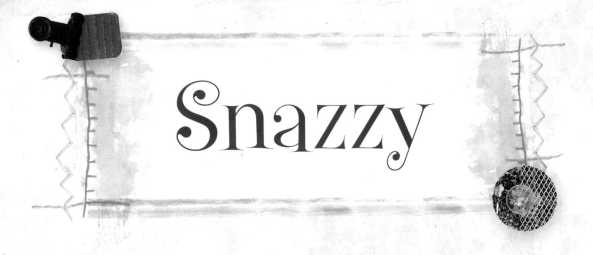

CHAPTER FOUR

Snazzy

Paper is the base for every scrapbook layout. It's the most essential supply to have on hand and the one that surrounds any scrapbooker. While basic, it is far from plain—with its multi-hued patterns and subtle textures—and arguably the most versatile supply in any collection. Stamp it, tear it, cut it, piece it, sand it, stitch it, then add layers and dimension; do just about anything with paper and you'll create a snazzy page.

couldn't reach the pedals
couldn't make it go,
loved dad's old bike,
loved to climb on up,
just sat in the seat,
could sit there all day,
riding, coasting, zooming,
flying fast away.

red
BIKE

Stamped and Painted Transparencies

the Story

mouse

Ralphie and the

it was a long time com
a long time to wait,
waited his whole long
Ralphie finally
had his moment,
a quarrel, a struggle,
a final hurrah,
his legendary strife;
the yard was golden
in the last light of the c
he stepped out of his t
bravely into the comin
stalwart old bag of bor
and i imagine
he was strong
and he was proud,
stalked the garden
mercilessly,
tracked that mouse
across the yard,
and he fought clean
and he fought hard;
and into the night there
cry of the old boy
returned from battle,
that cry shook our bon
made windows rattle,
piercing into the fallen
calling to the exultant s
Ralphie stood fluffy triu
in the end,
stood straight and tall
with sly blink-blink to g
defeated mouse lay at
crowning glory on
his c. vitae,
memorialised his last t
18 years and proud her
remembered for always
for all to know.

TRANSPARENCIES ARE SUCH A WONDERFUL ADDITION TO YOUR COLLECTION OF SUPPLIES, and being able to stamp and color them with vibrant inks makes them that much more fun. Alcohol inks or watercolors made for film paint on smoothly and cling to the transparency, drying quickly. I love the almost theatrical feel these stamped pieces can give to a layout, setting the stage for a great story.

PAGE SUPPLY LIST

Cardstock; patterned paper (7gypsies, Autumn Leaves, Prima); velvet paper; letter stickers (Making Memories); gesso (Tri-Art); watercolor paint (Winsor & Newton); watercolor paint for film (Dr. Ph. Martin); ink (Stewart Superior); stamps (Autumn Leaves, Creative Imaginations, Purple Onion); rub-on accents (K&Co., Scrapworks); clip; photo corners (Canson, Heidi Swapp); fibers (BasicGrey); floss (DMC); decorative scissors (Provo Craft)

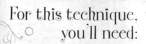

For this technique, you'll need:

Transparency sheets

Stamps

Solvent or hybrid ink

Watercolor paint and brushes or alcohol inks

1 APPLY THE STAMP

Stamp your image onto the rough side of the transparency with solvent ink or hybrid ink. Let the ink set to dry.

2 FILL IN WITH COLOR

Color the side of the image that you stamped with transparent watercolor or alcohol inks. These inks won't bead up on the transparency like other liquid inks can. Let the ink dry, then cut out the shapes to use as embellishments on the page.

Fun Dots

Simple stamped circles filled with vibrant inks dot this page and lend the entire layout a feeling of playfulness and youth—just perfect for capturing this moment of my favorite great-aunt on the floor playing with my daughters.

99

PAGE SUPPLY LIST

Cardstock; watercolor paint for film (Dr. Ph. Martin); transparency; stamps (Creative Imaginations); buttons (Autumn Leaves); photo corners (Heidi Swapp); floss (DMC); rub-on accents (KI Memories); pen and ink (Speedball)

Dimensional Additions

Once b pon
b cbsi on
b Hill

she knew in
her heart she
was a true
princess, and the
story she told
started once upon
a castle on
a hill.

I AM ALWAYS LOOKING FOR NEW WAYS TO ADD DIMENSION to my projects. I found that a plastic box, which once held sheets of chipboard shapes, would be a great addition to my layout. The box was the perfect size and thickness for attaching to the back of the page and holding some trinkets. Adding mesh to the hole in my photo adds an air of secrecy as it guards the contents of the heart.

PAGE SUPPLY LIST

Cardstock; patterned paper (Anna Griffin, NRN Designs, unknown handmade); rhinestones, wire (Westrim); gesso (Tri-Art); watercolor paint and paper (Winsor & Newton); floss (DMC); wire mesh (Making Memories); button, rub-on accents (Autumn Leaves); fabric stars; label (Making Memories); flower (Prima); pen and ink (Speedball)

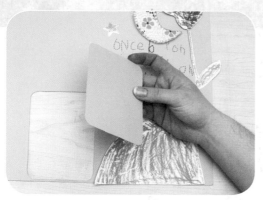

For this technique, you'll need:

Cardstock

Clear, plastic box

Craft knife

Glue dots

Patterned or painted paper

Small trinkets

Tape

Mesh

1 PICK THE PLACEMENT

With a craft knife, cut a hole in the background cardstock where the clear plastic box will be placed. Make sure the hole is smaller than the box opening.

2 ATTACH THE BOX

Back your box with patterned or painted paper. Place small trinkets (like the sparkly crown I used) inside. Then place glue dots around the perimeter of the box and adhere the box to the cardstock.

3 ADD MESH TO THE HOLE

Cut out a section of your page (such as this heart cut from the photo on my layout). Attach mesh to the back of the page with tape, covering the hole. Place the hole over the box. Secure the page to the cardstock.

Fresh Borders

it was her 7th birthday
and all the girls came,
to eat birthday cake
and play party games;
pink plastic baskets,
pink paper frills,
pink candy favours,
played pin-the-tail;
her best friend came,
her best friend was there,
signed her card
to Carol A.L.
from Donna M.C.
46 birthdays pass,
seems too quickly,
now,
no more party dresses,
no more party hats,
she has that card
in the jam cupboard
still good friends
after all these years.

PAPER HATS AND PARTY DRESSES

1961

7

SEEING ALL THE COUNTLESS PRE-CUT BORDERS in expected patterns available may make you think borders are rather boring or outdated as a page element, but they don't have to be. Repeat any pattern across your page, and you've got a border. And don't be limited by placement: borders may commonly wrap neatly around a central portion of a layout, but they can also be stretched or stacked in whatever manner best suits your page.

PAGE SUPPLY LIST

Patterned paper (Crate Paper); tissue paper; vellum (Autumn Leaves); floss (DMC); clips, vellum tags (Making Memories); rub-ons (7gypsies, Autumn Leaves, Fancy Pants, K&Co.); flowers (Prima); buttons (Autumn Leaves); string; tags (Heidi Grace); brads (Making Memories); pen and ink (Speedball)

FLOWER POWER

Thread three strands of embroidery floss onto a needle. Cut the petals from a silk flower. Stack six petals together and poke the needle near the tip of the petal stack. Pull the flowers onto the thread. Repeat to create five bunches of flowers. Wrap the embroidery floss around to the back of the layout and secure it with tape. Note: I didn't secure the flower bunches with a tied knot, but you can if you'd like.

FUN FLAGS

Cut a 2.5-inch (6.5cm) wide strip of two-ply tissue paper. Fold the plys in half to get a 1.25-inch (3cm) strip. Unfold the strip and place a string into the crease. Run a line of tacky glue below the string and fold the tissue paper over to trap the string. Cut triangles out to create the flags.

BUTTON UP

Thread a thick cotton string onto an embroidery needle. Stack a small button onto a large button. Thread the needle through the front of the button stack, and then from the back to the front. Tie a knot at the front of the buttons to secure them in place.

STACKED STRIPS

Cut a piece of vellum into an irregular wave shape. Cut horizontal strips from the wave. Stack six of the strips, and thread them onto embroidery floss, as shown for the flower border (above).

For this technique, you'll need:

Embroidery floss
Needle
Silk flowers
Tape
Two-ply tissue paper
Thick cotton string
Tacky glue
Scissors
Small and large buttons
Vellum

103

Sanding
over Chipboard

IT'S NATURAL TO ADD WORDS, SHAPES AND OTHER DESIGNS to a layout using color. But for a change of pace, why not try taking it away? By placing bulky items under white-core cardstock and sanding away the surface color, you can add elements to your page in the form of negative images, and create a truly positive design.

PAGE SUPPLY LIST

Cardstock; chipboard (Making Memories, Maya Road); watercolor paint (Winsor & Newton); buttons (Autumn Leaves); photo corners (Heidi Swapp); sandpaper; pen and ink (Speedball)

1 ADD PAINTED COLOR IF DESIRED

Spatter watercolor paint in a coordinating color onto white-core cardstock. (The cardstock may be colored, but the core needs to be white for this technique.) Allow the paint to dry.

For this technique, you'll need:

Cardstock with a white core

Watercolor paint and brush (optional)

Scissors

Chipboard letters and stars

Rough grit sandpaper

2 SAND THE SURFACE, REVEALING THE WHITE

Cut the cardstock into blocks sized to fit the chipboard letters. Place a chipboard letter under the cardstock. Holding the letter firmly in place with one finger, sand the surface of the cardstock, paying careful attention around the edges to create a clearly defined image.

The Sanded Page

Sanding over patterned paper is an easy way to create your own custom-distressed paper. I used the stencil portion of chipboard shapes to create the flourish above the photo and some of the flowers on this layout. I used regular chipboard pieces to sand the photo corners and other flowers.

105

PAGE SUPPLY LIST

Patterned paper (Rouge de Garance); chipboard (BasicGrey, Fancy Pants, Maya Road); buttons (Autumn Leaves); rhinetones (Westrim); photo corners (Canson); pen (Sakura)

Contact Paper Transfer

106

IN A CONTACT PAPER TRANSFER, the toner from a laser copy is left bonded to the sticky back side of the contact paper. The resulting image is reversed from the original. The still-adhesive nature of the paper after the transfer process makes selective coloring or patterning of the image very simple. This technique also works with packing tape.

PAGE SUPPLY LIST

Cardstock; contact paper; patterned paper (Autumn Leaves, K&Co., Scenic Route); rub-ons (Autumn Leaves, Heidi Grace); letter stickers (Making Memories); artist's crayons (Caran d'Ache); embroidered flourish (Autumn Leaves); decorative scissors (Provo Craft); stamp (Creative Imatinations); floss (DMC); ink (Stewart Superior)

For this technique, you'll need:

Laser printout

Clear contact paper

Scissors

Rag and warm water

Patterned paper

Craft knife

Clear glue (optional)

1 COPY THE IMAGE AND CUT THE CONTACT PAPER

Make a print or copy of your image using a laser printer. Cut a piece of clear contact paper and place it over the image, peeling the paper backing off slowly as you go.

2 RUB AWAY THE PAPER BACKING

Wet a rag with warm water, wringing it out just a bit. Lay the rag over the back of the image to wet the paper. Use the cloth to rub the paper from the contact paper. This process takes a bit of time and elbow grease, but be patient and keep at it.

3 COMPLETE THE TRANSFER

Once all the paper is rubbed off, the back side will be matte and tacky. The front will be shiny.

4 ADD PATTERN TO SELECT AREAS

For this layout, I wanted to place patterned paper behind the image transfer for a hint of color. To do this, reverse the image and print it on the back side of the patterned paper. Cut out the elements you want to be colored (in this case, the jacket and pants), using the image on the patterned paper as a guide. Place the patterned paper shapes behind the transfer. The transfer should be tacky enough to stick to your layout; if it's not, use a clear glue to adhere.

107

Matte Gel Transfer

IMAGE TRANSFERS DONE WITH MATTE GEL are versatile and quite easy to do. Matte gel, an acrylic polymer, bonds to the ink on a laser-copied image as the gel dries, and the two are then fully bonded together on the transfer surface. The image can be applied to a variety of surfaces including wood, fabric, canvas, paper, cardstock and glass. Note that white areas of images will actually be transparent in the transfer, allowing you to experiment with layering images, as I have done in this layout with a photo of my grandfather and an old map of Europe.

PAGE SUPPLY LIST

Cardstock; gesso, matte gel, paint (Tri-Art); fabric (unknown); chipboard letters (Maya Road); stamps (Magnetic Poetry); walnut ink (FiberScraps); labels (7gypsies, Li'l Davis); rub-ons (7gypsies); photo corners (Anna Griffin, Heidi Swapp); tag, twill (Autumn Leaves); fabric tape (7gypsies); masking tape

1 LAYER MEDIUM ON A LASER COPY

Use a large flat brush to spread a thin, even layer of matte gel directly onto a laser copy of a vintage map.

2 APPLY THE MAP TO GESSOED FABRIC

While the gel is still wet, firmly press the map face down onto gesso-treated fabric backed with cardstock. Use a brayer to set the image into place. Let it dry.

3 REVEAL THE TRANSFER

Dampen the map with water until the paper appears translucent. Wet a rag with warm water, then use the rag to rub away the paper, revealing the transferred image.

4 TRANSFER ANOTHER IMAGE

Apply a second transfer over the first if you like, using the same technique.

For this technique, you'll need:

Laser copied images for transfer (vintage map, portrait)

Matte gel acrylic medium

Large flat brush

Fabric adhered to cardstock, treated with gesso

Brayer

Rag and warm water

109

Technique Tip

When applying matte gel to an image, I often use my fingers, as I find this creates a much more even layer than a paintbrush.

Stamp Masking

By using a simple masking technique and stamping, you can easily create a pictorial background or decorative title block for your layout. I sometimes find stamping to be limiting—especially when trying to strike the correct balance of contrast between paper and stamping ink—but with masking, the background can easily be filled in with additional stamping or even by direct-to-paper inking.

PAGE SUPPLY LIST

Cardstock; patterned paper (Autumn Leaves, Scenic Route); stamps (Autumn Leaves, Ma Vinci); ink (Clearsnap, Stewart Superior); brads (Autumn Leaves, Making Memories); photo corners (Heidi Swapp); pen and ink (Speedball)

1 STAMP AND TRACE

Stamp your design onto cardstock. For my page, I stamped grass, stems and leaves. Place a piece of regular copy paper over the stamping and trace over the design.

2 APPLY THE LETTER MASKS

Cut out the traced design, leaving a small margin around the stamped image. Secure it over the stamped image on the cardstock with a tiny bit of glue stick. This will mask the stamped design from the background stamping in steps 3 and 4. Print and cut out the letters for the title. Use a dab of glue stick to secure these to the white cardstock as well.

3 STAMP ON THE COLOR

Use the entire inkpad to stamp color onto the cardstock and over the masks. Apply extra color around the title area to make sure it pops when the masks are removed.

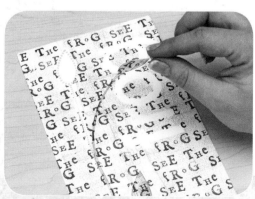

4 FINISH THE BACKGROUND AND REMOVE THE MASKS

If you like, stamp a phrase or anything else onto the background as well. When done, remove the masks and any remaining adhesive.

For this technique, you'll need:

Cardstock (white or light-colored)

Stamps (grass, stems, leaves, small alphabet)

Ink pads (light and dark green, light and dark blue)

Scissors

Copy paper

Glue stick

Printed letters

Hand-Cut Elements

HAND-CUTTING PAGE ELEMENTS WAS ONE OF THE FIRST TECHNIQUES I really fell in love with. The ability to customize any title or shape to any size, color or pattern is absolutely addictive! Try layering and combining elements to create your own unique page design.

PAGE SUPPLY LIST

Cardstock; patterned paper (Autumn Leaves, Crate Paper, K&Co., KI Memories, Making Memories, Prima, Rhonna Designs); vellum (Canson); brushes (Designfruit); photo corners (Heidi Swapp); Haettenscheweiler font (Internet download)

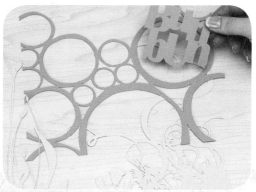

For this technique,
you'll need:

Cardstock

*Computer-generated
designs or clipart*

Craft knife

Liquid glue

Toothpick

1 PRINT AND CUT THE CENTERS

Create a design on your computer or find a clipart image. Print the design onto the back of cardstock, reversing the images so that they will face correctly when they are cut out. Begin cutting by removing the centers of any shapes or letters.

2 CUT THE ROUNDED PARTS

Cut out the other rounded areas next, leaving the straight edges intact.

3 MOVE ON TO THE STRAIGHT LINES

Finish by cutting all the straight lines.

4 HANDCUT ADDITIONAL ELEMENTS

Cut additional elements, like circles and flowers, in the same manner. Apply liquid glue to the letters using a toothpick and attach the letters to your page.

113

Paper Mosaic

MOSAICS ARE TRADITIONALLY CREATED USING TILES set into plaster, but for scrapbooking we can simplify the whole process down to paper and glue. The homemade look of mosaics—using squares cut from a variety of paper textures and finishes—can give visual interest to an otherwise plain layout. Hand-cutting the paper tiles for random and irregular edges adds to the page's appeal.

PAGE SUPPLY LIST

Cardstock; textured paper (FiberMark); photo corners, vellum (Canson); old book page; corrugated paper (DMD); letter accents (K&Co.); snowflake sequins (unknown); floss (DMC)

For this technique,
you'll need:

Assorted papers

Scissors

Ruler

Glue stick

1 GATHER PAPERS

Collect an assortment of papers.
For the wintry theme on my layout,
I selected vellums, corrugated paper,
an old book page and textured paper
in a monochromatic color scheme.

2 CUT AND PASTE

Cut the papers into half-inch (1cm)
strips. Then, using a ruler to roughly
guide your cuts, snip the strips into
approximate half-inch (1cm) squares.

How you group or individually
place the squares will depend on the
layout, but be sure to uniformly
space the pieces apart to resemble
a mosaic before gluing them down.
Snowflake sequins centered on the
occasional square help maintain a
clean, linear look for the page while
adding a fun thematic touch.

115

More Than Just a Background

Don't stop at making a monochromatic
paper mosaic background. Use squares in
a color that contrasts with the background
to create a journaling block, as I did here.
I cut and placed the paper squares first,
then handwrote my journaling and
finished the page by adding letters and
a snowflake accent.

Paper Piecing

I LOVE PIECING TOGETHER WHIMSICAL AND FANTASTICAL BACKGROUNDS to house my photos and set the stage for my story. Paper piecing does not have to be limited to cute critters from coloring book pages; you can create any scene that comes to mind. I enjoy combining freehand cut pieces and leftover scraps for a truly eclectic look, and adding dimensional items for texture and interest.

PAGE SUPPLY LIST

Cardstock; patterned paper (Daisy D's); brads, clips, letters, tags (Making Memories); watercolor paint (Winsor & Newton); decorative scissors (Provo Craft); photo corners (Canson, Heidi Swapp); pen and ink (Speedball)

DESIGN, THEN FIND

Make a quick sketch of the design you'd like
to piece with paper, or find an image that
you'd like to use. Then go through your
papers—especially leftover scraps—and find
pieces that are similar to the shapes in your
design. Improvise using the shapes of the
scraps as they are instead of cutting them
exactly to the shapes in your sketch. For this
layout, I chose scraps from paper I had used
to make paper lanterns. Then glue your
paper pieces to your layout, following the
design sketch.

Simple yet Spectacular

In this layout, a very simple piecing of
two bittersweet berries and a whimsical
snow-covered hill makes a big impact on
the page.

PAGE SUPPLY LIST

*Cardstock; patterned paper (BasicGrey);
rub-on accent (Chatterbox); brads
(Autumn Leaves, Making Memories);
metal mesh (Making Memories); button
(Autumn Leaves); scissors (Provo Craft);
mylar; stamps (Magnetic Poetry); photo
corners (Canson); floss (DMC); pen
(Sakura); ink (Clearsnap)*

117

Homemade Letters

EVEN WITH THE OVERWHELMING VARIETY OF LETTERS AVAILABLE in scrapbooking stores today, I still sometimes enjoy fashioning my own out of whatever I have on hand. A pile of wire pieces can form a "T"; a curl of fibers could make an "E." You can easily customize homemade letters to fit your page theme, and they are a great way to use up those scraps that accumulate around your work space.

PAGE SUPPLY LIST

Cardstock; patterned paper (7gypsies); fibers (Maya Road); button (Autumn Leaves); photo corners (Heidi Swapp); wire (Westrim); rub-ons (My Mind's Eye); vellum, floss (DMC); pen (Sakura)

1 MAKE THE "P" AND "A"

Piece together the "P" from a rusty nail and a bottlecap backed with vellum. Freehand cut the arc of the "A" from a length of pink lace. Use pink fabric, ribbon and stitching to form the rest of the letter.

2 FORM THE "R" AND "E"

Freehand cut an "R" from fabric, and glue it onto white felt with a glue stick. If you like, stitch around the edges randomly and add a button for the hole. For the "E," cut a circle of blue cardstock and use the couching stitch (see page 80) to create the letter with long fibers.

3 FINISH WITH "N," "T" AND "S"

Cut a computer-generated "N" from white cardstock; adhere stripes of corrugated paper if desired. Twist together several lengths of blue wire to form the two lines of the "T." Freehand cut the "S" from fabric.

For this technique, you'll need:

Cardstock (blue, white)

Rusty nail

Bottlecap

Vellum

Lace (large pink, small white)

Scissors

Assorted fabrics

Ribbon

Needle

Embroidery floss

White felt

Glue stick

Button (optional)

Assorted fibers

Corrugated paper (optional)

Blue wire

Hand-Lettered Title

IF YOU ARE LIKE ME AND NOT ESPECIALLY FOND OF YOUR OWN HANDWRITING, this method is so simple and foolproof that you'll be surprised at just how lovely words written by your hand can be. By sketching quickly and repeatedly, then working in the fine detail, you can combine the spontaneity of a first draft with the polish of a final one.

PAGE SUPPLY LIST

Cardstock; watercolor paint and paper (Winsor & Newton); decorative scissors (Provo Craft); patterned paper (Scenic Route); buttons (MOD); tags (Making Memories); photo corners (American Crafts); rhinestones (Westrim); floss (DMC); pen and ink (Speedball)

For this technique, you'll need:

Cardstock or watercolor paper

Pencil

Eraser

Pen

Watercolor paint

Brush

1 WRITE LOOSELY AND QUICKLY

Cut cardstock or watercolor paper into the desired shape. Sketch out the area in which you'd like to place the title. Loosely hold the pencil and quickly write the word.

2 REWRITE IT

Quickly, before you have time to think, write the word again, going from the last letter to the first. Don't try to follow the letters exactly, just rewrite the word.

3 CLEAN UP AND ENHANCE

Clean up the letters with a pencil, making the lines more pronounced, and erasing some of the wayward lines outside the letterforms.

4 FINALIZE THE LETTERS

Finally, still with the pencil, add serifs, curls and swirls as you like. Then outline the letters in ink, erase the pencil lines and fill in the letters with color. Here, I filled the letters with watercolor paint, using the light, sketchy lines as a guide for painting with different colors. The same technique can be used for block letters.

121

Collage

COLLAGE, FROM THE FRENCH WORD *COLLÉ* MEANING "GLUE," involves adhering layers of paper together. At first glance, collage may seem overwhelming, but it's not if you take it one layer at a time. Archive-safe, artist-quality matte gel acrylic medium is a perfect adhesive for creating collage, and it dries to a toothy surface able to accept paint, ink and other wet media. For added interest, top a collage with dimensional objects.

PAGE SUPPLY LIST

Cardstock; matte gel (Tri-Art); letter stickers (Making Memories); paint (Curry's, Tri-Art); artist's crayons (Caran d'Ache); stamp (Sugarloaf); metal washers; microscope slides; rings; ink (Stewart Superior); pen (Sakura)

1 PREPARE COLLAGE ELEMENTS

Prepare two laser-copied images for matte gel transfer (see page 108). Place one image down on a transparency. Place the second image down directly on the background cardstock. Rub the papers off both transfers with warm water and a rag. On the second transfer, only the matte gel and the transfer will remain.

2 PAINT THE COLLAGE BACKGROUND

Paint the background of the collage. When I did my transfer on the transparency, the paper did not peel off as well as I would have liked, so I backed the image with white gesso to brighten the transfer.

3 BUILD LAYERS

Use acrylic paint to adhere the transparency. Then affix letter stickers. Use artist's crayons to fill with color and to add pattern to the background of the transfered images.

4 ADD DIMENSION

Using matte gel or acrylic paint, apply dimensional items like washers, gears and metal rings. Also add smaller images, in this case of the human heart. Using matte gel as adhesive, cover some of the images with microscope slides.

For this technique, you'll need:

Cardstock
Two laser-copied images
Matte gel acrylic medium
Clear transparency
Rag and warm water
White gesso
Acrylic paint (red, yellow)
Photo printed on transparency
Letter stickers
Artist's crayons
Metal rings, gears and washers
Small images
Microscope slides

123

Source Guide

The following companies manufacture products featured in this book. Please check your local retailers to find these materials, or go to a company's Web site for the latest product. In addition, we have made every attempt to properly credit the items mentioned in this book. We apologize to any company that we have listed incorrectly, and we would appreciate hearing from you.

7gypsies
(877) 749-7797
www.sevengypsies.com

Aleene's/Duncan Enterprises
(800) 438-6226
www.aleenes.com

American Crafts
(801) 226-0747
www.americancrafts.com

Anna Griffin, Inc.
(888) 817-8170
www.annagriffin.com

Artool - see Iwata Medea, Inc.

Autumn Leaves
(800) 588-6707
www.autumnleaves.com

BasicGrey
(801) 544-1116
www.basicgrey.com

Bazzill Basics Paper
(480) 558-8557
www.bazzillbasics.com

Blue Moon Beads
(800) 377-6715
www.bluemoonbeads.com

Canson, Inc.
(800) 628-9283
www.canson-us.com

Caran d'Ache
www.carandache.ch

Chatterbox, Inc.
(888) 416-6260
www.chatterboxinc.com

Christine Adolf Designs
www.christineadolf.com

Clearsnap, Inc.
(888) 448-4862
www.clearsnap.com

Craf-T Products
www.craf-tproducts.com

Crate Paper
(801) 798-8996
www.cratepaper.com

Crayola
(800) 272-9652
www.crayola.com

Creative Imaginations
(800) 942-6487
www.cigift.com

Curry's Art Store
(800) 268-2969
www.currys.com

Daisy D's Paper Company
(888) 601-8955
www.daisydspaper.com

Designfruit
www.designfruit.com

DMC Corp.
(973) 589-0606
www.dmc-usa.com

DMD Industries, Inc.
(800) 727-2727
www.dmdind.com

Doodlebug Design Inc.
(877) 800-9190
www.doodlebug.ws

Dr. Ph. Martin's
(800) 843-8293
www.docmartins.com

Fancy Pants Designs, LLC
(801) 779-3212
www.fancypantsdesigns.com

FiberMark
(802) 257-0365
www.fibermark.com

Fiber Scraps
(215) 230-4905
www.fiberscraps.com

Fiskars, Inc.
(866) 348-5661
www.fiskars.com

Heidi Grace Designs, Inc.
(866) 348-5661
www.heidigrace.com

Heidi Swapp/Advantus Corporation
(904) 482-0092
www.heidiswapp.com

Iwata Medea, Inc.
(503) 253-7308
www.iwata-medea.com

K&Company
(888) 244-2083
www.kandcompany.com

Karen Foster Design
(801) 451-9779
www.karenfosterdesign.com

Karen Russell
www.karenrussell.typepad.com

Krylon
(800) 457-9566
www.krylon.com

Leave Memories
www.leavememories.com

Li'l Davis Designs
(480) 223-0080
www.lildavisdesigns.com

Liquitex Artist Materials
(888) 422-7954
www.liquitex.com

Ma Vinci's Reliquary
www.reliquary.cyberstamps.com

Magic Mesh
(651) 345-6374
www.magicmesh.com

Magnetic Poetry
(800) 370-7697
www.magneticpoetry.com

Making Memories
(801) 294-0430
www.makingmemories.com

Marvy Uchida/
Uchida of America, Corp.
(800) 541-5877
www.uchida.com

May Arts
(800) 442-3950
www.mayarts.com

Maya Road, LLC
(214) 488-3279
www.mayaroad.com

Microsoft Corporation
www.microsoft.com

MOD — My Own Design
(303) 641-8680
www.mod-myowndesign.com

Mustard Moon
(763) 493-5157
www.mustardmoon.com

My Mind's Eye, Inc.
(800) 665-5116
www.mymindseye.com

NRN Designs
(800) 421-6958
www.nrndesigns.com

Nunn Designs
(800) 761-3557
www.nunndesign.com

Pebbles Inc.
(801) 235-1520
www.pebblesinc.com

Prima Marketing, Inc.
(909) 627-5532
www.primamarketinginc.com

Provo Craft
(800) 937-7686
www.provocraft.com

Purple Onion Designs
www.purpleoniondesigns.com

Ranger Industries, Inc.
(800) 244-2211
www.rangerink.com

Rhonna Designs
www.rhonnadesigns.com

Sakura Hobby Craft
(310) 212-7878
www.sakuracraft.com

Scenic Route Paper Co.
(801) 225-5754
www.scenicroutepaper.com

Scrapworks, LLC
(801) 363-1010
www.scrapworks.com

SEI, Inc.
(800) 333-3279
www.shopsei.com

Soft Flock/DonJer Products Corp.
(800) 336-6537
www.donjer.com

Speedball Art Products Company
(800) 898-7224
www.speedballart.com

Stewart Superior Corporation
(800) 558-2875
www.stewartsuperior.com

Stix2Anything
www.stix2fantastak.com

Sugarloaf Products, Inc.
(770) 484-0722
www.sugarloafproducts.com

Technique Tuesday, LLC
(503) 644-4073
www.techniquetuesday.com

Tri-Art
www.tri-art.ca

Westrim Crafts
(800) 727-2727
www.westrimcrafts.com

Winsor & Newton
www.winsornewton.com

Wrights Ribbon Accents
(877) 597-4448
www.wrights.com

Yupo Corporation
(888) 873-9876
www.yupo.com

Index

Discover more unique and creative ideas with these Memory Makers Books

See what's coming up from Memory Makers Books by checking out our blog: WWW.MEMORYMAKERSMAGAZINE.COM/BOOKSBLOG/

Step-by-step instructions on a variety of techniques show you how to create engaging, interactive pages that beg to be touched.

ISBN-13: 978-1-59963-018-2
ISBN-10: 1-59963-018-4
paperback   128 pages   Z1679

Push the boundaries of your scrapbooking with creative inspiration and innovative ideas from leading scrapbook designers Jodi Amidei and Torrey Scott.

ISBN-13: 978-1-59963-009-0
ISBN-10: 1-59963-009-5
paperback 128 pages Z0795

Learn from scrapbook artist Trudy Sigurdson ways to infuse textural themes from photographs into scrapbook art using textiles, metals, natural elements, art mediums, paper and clear elements.

ISBN-13: 978-1-59963-005-2
ISBN-10: 1-59963-005-2
paperback 128 pages Z0715

Take your art to a new level and explore new themes with the mix of thoughtful, evocative and funny Dares from authors Kristina Contes, Meghan Dymock, Nisa Fiin and Genevieve Simmonds.

ISBN-13: 978-1-59963-013-7
ISBN-10: 1-59963-013-3
paperback 128 pages Z1041

These books and other fine Memory Makers titles are available at your local scrapbook or craft store, bookstore or from online suppliers, including www.memorymakersmagazine.com.